A love of Mozart, a pair of scissors and some black paper are all that is needed for the magic of Lotte Reiniger as she creates some of her greatest masterpieces.

Here, in order of their appearance on stage, are some of the dramatic moments from *The Marriage of Figaro, Don Giovanni, Così fan tutte* and *The Magic Flute.*

Music: Wolfgang Amadeus Mozart
Libretto: Lorenzo Da Ponte and Emanuel Schikaneder
Scenery and costumes: Lotte Reiniger

La vendetta, oh la vendetta! Non so più cosa son

Susanna, il ciel vi salvi Voi che sapete che cos

Fermatevi... sentite... sortire ella non può

Che soave zeffiretto questa sera spirerà...

osa faccio... Susanna, tu mi sembri agitata e confusa

amor   Venite, inginocchiatevi: restate fermo lì

Vedrò mentre io sospiro, felice un servo mio!

Il biglietto...   Eccomi a' vostri piedi...

Ah… soccorso!… son tradito! Ah! chi mi dice m

Là ci darem la mano, là mi dirai di sì…

Deh vieni alla finestra, o mio tesoro

Non mi dir, bell'idol mio, che son io crudel con te

...l barbaro dov'è...   Madamina, il catalogo è questo...

Batti, batti, o bel Masetto, la tua povera Zerlina...

Mi tradì quell'alma ingrata...

Pentiti, cangia vita: è l'ultimo momento!

Ah, guarda, sorella, se bocca più bella...

Di pasta simile son tutti quanti...

Ah, che tutta in un momento si cangiò la sorte mia

Un contratto nuziale! Ah signor, son rea di morte...

Smanie implacabili che m'agitate...

Alla bella Despinetta vi presento, amici miei...

E nel tuo, nel mio bicchiero si sommerga...

Te lo credo, gioia bella, ma la prova far non vo'.

Zu Hilfe! Zu Hilfe! Sonst bin ich verloren...

He Sklaven! Legt ihr Fesseln an!

Alles fühlt der Liebe Freuden...   Ach, i

Ein Mädchen oder Weibchen wünscht Papageno si

Ich kann nichts tun als dich beklagen...

Er ist's. Sie ist's! Ich glaub es kaum!

l's, es ist verschwunden, ewig hin der Liebe Glück!

Pa-Pa-Pa-Pa-Papageno! Pa-Pa-Pa-Pa-Papagena!

CONTENTS

MOZART
THE REAL AMADEUS

Michel Parouty

THAMES AND HUDSON

On 27 January 1756 a powdery snow was steadily falling on Salzburg. In no. 9 Getreidegasse, Leopold Mozart was pacing up and down like a caged animal. From the next room he could hear muffled sounds of footsteps and whispering: his beloved wife Anna Maria was about to give birth to their seventh child... It was a boy. They called him Wolfgang.

CHAPTER 1

A CHILD PRODIGY
AT THE COURTS
OF EUROPE

The Mozart family occupied one floor of a large house in the Getreidegasse, seen here in an engraving from the 19th century when it was already a place of pilgrimage. Right: Mozart sentimentalized, in porcelain.

$\mathcal{S}$alzburg in Mozart's time: a principality with about 10,000 inhabitants.

Leopold Mozart was thirty-seven when his son was born. His family were bookbinders in Augsburg, but he chose to take up music, first in the service of Count Thurn und Taxis; in 1743 he was appointed fourth violin in the orchestra of Prince-Archbishop Firmian of Salzburg, becoming court composer and finally vice-Kapellmeister (assistant director of music). He wrote prolifically, compositions which were functional, workmanlike and easy on the ear, but not distinguished enough to bring him fame. A certain renown came his way unexpectedly, though not undeservedly, with the publication in 1756 (the year of Wolfgang's birth) of his *Violin Method*, which was to remain a standard work of reference for many

* Leopold [opposite] was quite an average person, devoid of genius. But he possessed talent, and his treatise on violin playing and some of his church sonatas amply demonstrate the strong pedagogical influences that were to mark Wolfgang's early studies. Wolfgang's mother [left], though lively, even-tempered and imaginative, appears to have been somewhat passive and superficial, and we get no clear picture of her even from the later references by her children. *

Emmanuel Buenzod, 1930

generations to come. For forty years Leopold carried
out his duties faithfully, though he frequently
had cause to lament the ingratitude with
which his efforts were rewarded.

In 1747 he had married Anna Maria
Pertl, daughter of a civil servant. Their
marriage lasted through separations
and sorrows; Wolfgang was their
seventh child, and of the other six only
Maria Anna (nicknamed Nannerl)
survived the perils which surrounded
infancy in those days. She was four and a
half when her brother was born.

Their maternal grandfather had also
been a musician, and it was natural that
the two Mozart children should grow
up steeped in music. Leopold
educated his children
carefully. His lessons, though
serious, were varied and
stimulating; Wolfgang was
fascinated by mathematics.
Nannerl, at the age of
eight, began to learn the
harpsichord and her
brother listened.

At the age of three, little Wolfgang sits at his sister's harpsichord searching out notes 'which like each other'

His progress was phenomenal. He began to compose before he could write. As early as 1762, when barely six, he showed his first compositions to his father,

Nannerl aged eleven. Though herself a child prodigy, she was soon overshadowed by her younger brother. She married a baron and died in 1829.

who was quite overcome. The boy's precocious talent and desire to learn were beyond doubt. Much later Andreas Schachtner, a court trumpeter, recalled: 'One day Wolfgang was busy scribbling away. His father asked what he was writing. "A keyboard concerto; I've nearly finished the first part." Leopold looked dubiously at the clumsy, childish manuscript and

The suit of clothes worn by the six-year-old Mozart in this portrait was given him by the Empress Maria Theresa; it was a cast-off from the Archduke Maximilian.

marvelled: Wolfgang, already capable of intense concentration, was a musician through and through.

Naturally, such rare gifts had to be exploited, and the best way clearly was to travel.

In 1762 the family sets off on its travels, led by a Leopold keen to 'show the world a miracle'

Their first tour, to Munich, capital of Bavaria, is not documented. The second was to Vienna, capital of the Habsburg Empire.

Though Nannerl played the harpsichord brilliantly, it was her brother who stole the show, as countless anecdotes record. At Ips, during mass, the little boy crept into the organ loft and charmed the Franciscan monks with his playing. The Bishop of Passau had already asked to see him; Count Pálffy sang his praises after seeing him play in Linz.

By the time the family arrived in Vienna on 6 October, everyone was already agog to see the child prodigy. The Mozarts were immediately in demand at all the best houses. They had hardly been there a week when the Archduke Joseph, eldest son of the Empress, insisted that his mother grant the family an audience at the palace of Schönbrunn. Maria Theresa allowed the boy to jump into her lap, fling his arms round her neck and give her a big kiss.

The imperial court assembles to admire the two extraordinary children

The court went into raptures over the confident littleboy for whom nothing seemed too difficult, even playing on a keyboard concealed under a cloth.

At Schönbrunn, a little girl no older than Wolfgang helped him up when he fell over. 'That was very kind of you,' he said to her gratefully.

Opposite: Leopold Mozart watches his son attentively as he composes. In this scene imagined by a 19th-century artist, the visitor on the right is probably Schachtner, owner of a violin whose sweet full tone led the young Wolfgang to call it the 'butter violin'.

The violin Mozart had as a child.

At six Mozart had already mastered the basic techniques. On their journey to Vienna the family was exempted from paying the local customs dues, thanks to the little boy. 'For he at once made friends with the customs officer, showed him the square piano, invited him to visit us and played him a minuet on his little violin, and we were allowed through' (Leopold Mozart, letter of 16 October 1762).

Vienna, city of ceremonies

Gala performance in the Redoutensaal of the Hofburg (the imperial palace), on the occasion of the marriage of Archduke Joseph and Isabella of Parma in 1760. The marriage of a prince was a good pretext for sumptuous festivities, calculated to impress the people, who always loved celebrations. What could be more alluring than the prospect of employment in the capital of the Empire? In the figure of one of the boys in the front row we can imagine we see the six-year-old Mozart, who was to be welcomed at the Viennese court two years later.

Musical capital of Europe

Musical entertainment for the wedding feast of Joseph and Isabella. Seat of the Holy Roman Empire from 1558 to 1806, Vienna was a prosperous city whose population rose during the reign of Maria Theresa from 88,000 to 175,000. The Austrian capital was a city which was well known for welcoming all comers, including foreigners: this tradition lasted until well into the 20th century and was reflected in all branches of art. As centre of the Habsburg Empire it played host to the whole of Europe, especially during the Enlightenment. Vienna's exceptional vitality reached its climax at the end of the 18th century under the aegis of the imperial family and was manifested above all in the field of musical and artistic display.

'When I grow up I will marry you.' The girl was Marie Antoinette, future queen of France. It is not known how she responded to his proposal.

The schedule of concerts, receptions and invitations was hectic, and at the end of the second week Wolfgang had to retire to bed. He quickly recovered, but the pace had to slacken. Before long it was time to leave. On 5 January 1763, after a rewarding detour to Pressburg (Bratislava), the family reached home. They brought with them two sumptuous suits of clothes, both gifts from the Empress, and the satisfaction of instant fame. This was not to last. The excitement of the early days waned; and they were to find that the fickle Viennese public was quick to lose interest.

Even in the Age of Enlightenment, musicians are only servants, at the mercy of their masters

Soon after his return, Mozart was ill again. While convalescing he took the opportunity to polish his skills as a violinist. The start of 1763 saw the end of the Seven Years War; it was also the time when Leopold became vice-Kapellmeister at the Salzburg court, where Joseph Haydn's brother Michael (1737–1806) had recently been made Konzertmeister (leader and director of the orchestra). But 9 June

A bove left: the young Mozart at the Viennese court. 'We were there from 3 to 6 o'clock, and the Emperor himself... made me go and hear the Infanta play the violin' (Leopold Mozart, letter of 16 October 1762).

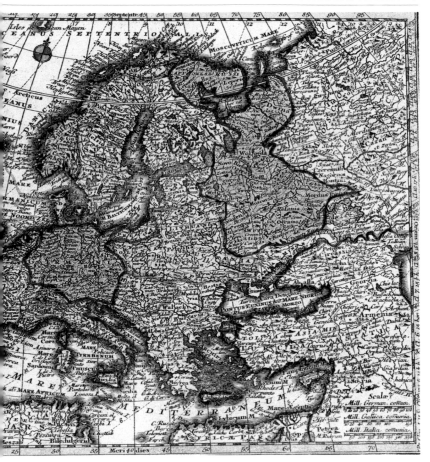

marked the beginning of a great odyssey which was to last three years. Leopold's letters give us a vivid insight into the life of a musician in the 18th century. It has little in common with the romantic vision of the artist alone in his ivory tower, living for his art; being unsalaried, the instrumentalist, singer or composer had to rely more on his own resources than on the generosity of princes. The presents he did receive (watches, snuff-boxes and so on; Mozart

Europe in the mid-18th century. Germany itself was made up of a multiplicity of small courts – a legacy of the Treaty of Westphalia which ended the Thirty Years War in 1648. Each had its own ruler and not all were enlightened.

soon had a fine collection) were not easy to turn into money and did not guarantee the daily bread.

From court to palace, father and son travel the roads of Europe

The family set off again. On the way to Munich they were held up by a broken wheel in Wasserburg, and Wolfgang astonished his audience by his cleverness at playing a pedal organ without having learnt the instrument. Finally they reached Munich and the court of Maximilian III, where they were well rewarded and given warm letters of recommendation.

At Augsburg, however, the first appearance of the two children before a large audience proved a disappointment. At Ludwigsburg, Duke Karl Eugen of Württemberg did not deign even to hear them, so besotted was he with the music of his own Kapellmeister, Nicola Jommelli. Fortunately they were more kindly treated by Karl Theodor, Elector Palatine, for whom they played at Schwetzingen; and in his summer residence they were lucky enough to hear the Mannheim orchestra – the best of the day. On they went, to Worms, Mainz and Frankfurt, where the young Goethe was in the audience. Later the poet was to reminisce about the 'little fellow with his wig and sword'. Koblenz and Bonn followed, then Cologne and Aachen, where Princess Amelia, sister of Frederick the Great, smothered Wolfgang with caresses – the only thing she was really generous with.

Augsburg in the 18th century, a centre of commerce and banking. Below: a flute-maker of Augsburg.

Opposite: Baron Grimm (1723–1807).

Several stops later they arrived in Brussels, which was then capital of the Austrian Netherlands and governed by Charles of Lorraine, brother of the Emperor Francis I. Finally, on 18 November 1763, the family arrived in Paris, where Count von Eyck, son-in-law of Count Arco, grand chamberlain at the Salzburg court, welcomed them in his residence, the Hôtel de Beauvais.

Wolfgang and the Marquise de Pompadour, January 1764.

In the French capital they meet a ministering angel: Baron von Grimm

Baron Christian Friedrich Melchior von Grimm, a passionate advocate of Italian music, had lived in France for thirty years. He was in with the French literary circles of the time and was chiefly known throughout Europe for his *Literary, Philosophical and Critical Correspondence*, a journal, circulated in manuscript, in which he described French intellectual life. An article he wrote on 11 December 1763 provided the best possible introduction: news of the Mozarts' arrival spread like wildfire, and the entire aristocracy, ever avid for novelty, became completely obsessed with them. At the end of December they were received at Versailles and smothered in embraces by most of the royal ladies, though not by Madame de Pompadour, to the sensitive Wolfgang's chagrin. On 1 January 1764 they were invited to the traditional banquet.

Tea with the Prince de Conti

This genre painting was executed by Michel Barthélemy Ollivier in the summer of 1766 during Mozart's second visit to Paris. It is set in the Mirror Room of the Palais du Temple, residence of the Prince de Conti. The ten-year-old Mozart is barely visible behind the harpsichord. Next to him stands the tenor Pierre Jélyotte, a great performer of Rameau's works; he was also a violinist and guitarist in the King's orchestra, and is seen here tuning his instrument. It is typical of 18th-century French society that the assembled company are paying little attention to the music but are carrying on with what they are doing, so that, as Mozart complained years later (again in Paris), he 'had to play to the chairs, tables and walls' (letter of 1 May 1778).

More important than any socializing, however, were their encounters with other musicians.

In Paris Wolfgang meets Johann Schobert, a German composer with whom he long remains in touch

Leopold asserted in a letter of 1–3 February 1764 that French and Italian music were in a perpetual state of war, and observed that the French taste of the moment was on its way out. But he also emphasized the importance of the Germans, including the harpsichordist Johann Gottfried Eckard of Augsburg, his colleague Johann Schobert (musical director for the Prince de Conti, whose fine orchestra boasted the cellist Jean Pierre Duport and the composer François Joseph Gossec), and Hermann Friedrich Raupach. Their talent had its influence on the young Mozart, who in 1767 took movements of sonatas by several of these composers and arranged them as harpsichord concertos.

The crucially important influence of Schobert is apparent in the works Mozart composed at that time, the two groups of sonatas for harpsichord with violin accompaniment, K.6–7 and K.8–9, published in Paris and dedicated respectively to Princess Victoire, daughter of Louis XV, and the Comtesse de Tessé, lady-in-waiting to the Dauphine. Whereas Eckard was first and foremost a harpsichord soloist, Schobert was a versatile musician, inventive and imaginative. His work, a blend of German, Italian and French influences, could hardly fail to

The first compositions of substance by the seven-year-old boy are a set of sonatas for harpsichord with violin accompaniment (K.6–7) written during the winter of 1763–4 (top). Above: a French harpsichord of 1716.

A concert (detail from an 18th-century painting). Towards the end of the 18th century the harpsichord was displaced in popularity by the pianoforte – in its first, wooden-framed form sometimes called a fortepiano. As a virtuoso performer Mozart appreciated the instruments of his day, and in 1777 he was quick to enthuse over the products of the Augsburg piano manufacturer Andreas Stein. Unlike the harpsichord, where the strings are plucked, the pianoforte (literally, 'soft-loud') has an action in which the strings are struck by hammers, which allows greater gradations of dynamics from 'pianissimo' (very soft) to 'fortissimo' (very loud), and a wide variety of touch. Further modifications led to the development of the modern piano.

have its effect on so receptive a young mind. But the time came to leave Paris.

In London Wolfgang discovers the sunshine of Italy in the music of Johann Christian Bach

On 10 April 1764 the family set off for Calais to take the boat to Dover, and on 23 April they arrived in London. Four days after their arrival, they were received by King George III and Queen Charlotte.

The relaxed atmosphere at the English court was most welcome after the formality of Versailles. On 19 May they gave a private concert to an appreciative royal family: in Buckingham House Wolfgang improvised, sight-read music by Georg Christoph Wagenseil, Karl Friedrich Abel, Johann Christian Bach and George Frideric Handel, accompanied the Queen's singing, and played the violin and organ.

In Paris the dominant musical atmosphere had been German, but in London it was Italian. Paradoxically, this was due to two Germans – partly to Abel, but chiefly to Johann Christian Bach, youngest son of the great Johann Sebastian, who became one of Wolfgang's closest friends.

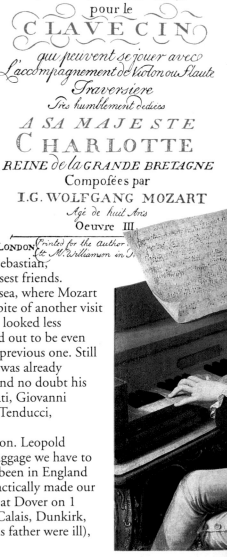

The summer was spent in Chelsea, where Mozart composed his first symphony. In spite of another visit to court, prospects for the autumn looked less exciting, but the new season turned out to be even more valuable artistically than the previous one. Still less than nine years old, Wolfgang was already thinking of composing an opera, and no doubt his encounters with two famous castrati, Giovanni Manzuoli and Giusto Ferdinando Tenducci, strengthened his determination.

But yet again they had to move on. Leopold lamented: 'The very sight of the luggage we have to pack makes me perspire. We have been in England for a whole year. Why, we have practically made our home here!' The family embarked at Dover on 1 August 1765 and passed through Calais, Dunkirk, Lille (where both Wolfgang and his father were ill), Ghent and The Hague.

The return journey includes several stops as the Mozarts are fêted everywhere

In the Netherlands Wolfgang performed for the Prince of Orange and his sister, Princess Caroline of Nassau-Weilburg. But Nannerl fell gravely ill with intestinal typhoid; Wolfgang continued composing until he too succumbed. Once they had recovered, the children gave two recitals in Amsterdam and took part in the installation celebrations for William V before paying another visit to Paris. There they stayed two months, during which Baron Grimm again acted as a wonderful press officer. Paris, Lyons, Geneva, Lausanne, Berne, Zurich… No longer did they need to ask to be invited! One slight worry was that they had been absent from Salzburg much longer than envisaged; but Prince-Archbishop Siegmund von Schrattenbach was wise enough to realize that the glory they acquired abroad would reflect on Salzburg too.

The Mozarts were back in their own home on 30 November 1766. During this first tour of the courts of Europe, the boy had not only become something of a legend, but had had musical experiences far beyond those of a mere child prodigy.

Johann Christian Bach (1735–82), portrayed here by Thomas Gainsborough, revealed to Mozart the beauties of a melodic style less austere than that of the Germans.

Left: the young Mozart at the piano, and the title page of a further set of sonatas. 'Now I have the heavy expense of having six sonatas of our Master Wolfgang engraved and printed, which (at her own request) are being dedicated to the Queen of Great Britain' (Leopold Mozart, letter of 27 November 1764).

Mozart was now eleven and famous, with an eventful life already behind him. He had grown out of being a child prodigy, and his task would be to show the world that, far from being merely a precocious brat, he was an outstanding musician. Within a few years he would be in Italy.

CHAPTER 2

FROM CHILD PRODIGY TO COMPOSER

In Italy the young Mozart (opposite) was enthusiastically received by the music-loving owners of houses like the Villa Albani (above).

Eleven can be an awkward age. But Mozart in 1767 was no ordinary child. He loved playing games, joking, being made a fuss of, but he also adored work. The few months spent in Salzburg before setting off on more travels were devoted to studying, and under Leopold's guidance he got down to it straight away. Music in London had been much influenced by Italy; now it was time to concentrate on Germany, and he turned his attention to Carl Philipp Emanuel Bach, Johann Joseph Fux, Johann Eberlin, Johann Adolf Hasse, and Handel.

Mozart was composing in three-part harmony, and he amused himself by giving names to each of the parts: *Signor d'Alto, Marchese Tenore, Duca Basso* (Sir Alto, Lord Tenor, His Grace the Bass). His working speed was phenomenal. On arrival the Prince-Archbishop, Count Siegmund von Schrattenbach, put him to the test to see if his reputation was deserved. Commissions promptly flooded in. He was asked to write an oratorio to be performed on 12 March 1767, called *Die Schuldigkeit des ersten Gebots* ('The Obligation of the First Commandment'), collaborating with Michael Haydn and the organist Anton Adlgasser, both much older than himself. This was followed by a Latin comedy, *Apollo and Hyacinthus*, written for a celebration at Salzburg University and performed in its Great Hall. In both works the conventional forms are permeated with Mozart's own uniquely personal warmth of expression.

Nine months passed, and then the whole family set out again, this time for Vienna.

The days of the 'miracle' are over. The stay in Vienna proves full of disappointments

Maria Theresa's daughter Maria Carolina was about to marry Ferdinand, King of Naples, and it looked as if an excited city might offer a wealth of attractive opportunities to musicians. Alas, fate intervened cruelly: an epidemic of smallpox carried off the young bride. (In any case the city's atmosphere had totally changed since the death of Francis I and the accession of the austere Joseph II.) Leopold's one desire was to get his family away as fast as possible. Too late: Wolfgang was struck down at Olmütz (Olomouc) in Bohemia, and Nannerl also fell ill. Mercifully they recovered, and on 10 January 1768 they all returned to Vienna, where they stayed for a year. But it was not an easy time. Wolfgang and his sister were now twelve and seventeen, and had lost the curiosity value they had had as children; yet the budding composer could not yet hope to compete with the great

Left and above: two composers famous in Mozart's lifetime – Carl Philipp Emanuel Bach (1714–88) and Johann Adolf Hasse (1699–1783). Originally a tenor, Hasse became a composer of Italian *opere serie*. He said of the young Mozart, 'One day this child will eclipse us all.'

names of the day, Joseph Haydn (1732–1809) and Christoph Willibald Gluck (1714–87). Mozart had his first taste of jealousy and rivalry.

To attract attention to his son, Leopold, with the Emperor's backing, urges him to write an opera

Wolfgang needed little encouragement to attempt an opera. A theatre impresario, 'Count' Affligio, offered a contract, but turned out to be a fraud, ending up in the galleys. Mozart did write the opera, *La finta semplice* (*The Sly Maiden*), to a libretto by Marco Coltellini based on a comedy by Carlo Goldoni, but the Viennese cabal kept it off the stage for a year; finally it was performed in Salzburg for the birthday of the Prince-Archbishop. This delay was a bitter disappointment for Mozart. Consolation came, however, from an unexpected quarter: a wealthy music-lover, Dr Franz Anton Mesmer (originator of the theory of animal magnetism), commissioned him to write a short opera for his private theatre. *Bastien and Bastienne* was premiered on 1 October 1768, in a friendly, intimate atmosphere which perfectly complemented its tale of rustic love-affairs.

Enthusiastic as ever, Wolfgang devours Italian operas and German symphonies

The final weeks of the stay in Vienna included another source of satisfaction for the youthful composer: the success of his first mass, the *Waisenhausmesse* ('Orphanage Mass'), K.139, written for the consecration of the new chapel of the court-sponsored orphanage. Leopold's letters tell proudly of its success, 'which has restored that reputation

Opposite: Mozart around the age of twelve is suggested by this portrait of an unknown musician.

•As for Wolfgang's opera [*La finta semplice*] all I can tell you is that...a whole hell of musicians has risen up to prevent the display of a child's ability. ... A conspiracy has been formed to produce it...extremely badly and thus ruin it.•
Leopold Mozart
14 September 1768

Christoph Willibald Gluck was at the height of his fame in 1768 after *Orfeo and Euridice* (1762) and *Alceste* (1767).

which our enemies, by preventing the performance of the opera, intended to destroy' (letter of 14 December 1768). All in all the material benefits of the journey were small, but they were offset by the musical ones: in those few months Mozart was able to hear several Italian operas, including Hasse's *Partenope*, Nicola Piccinni's *La buona figliuola* and Gluck's *Alceste* (which was to remain one of his favourites), and to absorb the new trends revolutionizing the German symphonic scene, whose leaders were Joseph Haydn, Johann Baptist Vanhal and Karl Ditters von Dittersdorf. These two contrasting but complementary traditions combined to form the aesthetic framework of his whole subsequent career.

Siegmund von Schrattenbach, Prince-Archbishop of Salzburg from 1753 to 1771.

At Salzburg, the Archbishop, growing impatient, suspended Leopold's salary; but he was a benevolent master, and welcomed them home warmly, putting Wolfgang in charge of his court orchestra as Konzertmeister and granting father and son fresh leave of absence.

On 11 December 1769 father and son set off for Italy

Nannerl, now eighteen, had become a fine teacher, and her lessons were bringing the household a substantial income, so while her brother and father visited Italy, she and her mother stayed at home.

Mozart was of a happy temperament, and his letters are full of gaiety – unsophisticated, enthusiastic, joky, and still very childish, oddly lacking the lightness of touch so characteristic of his music. 'Dearest Mamma! My heart is full of delight and pleasure, because I am so enjoying this journey; it is warm in the carriage and our coachman is a capital fellow who drives fast whenever the road gives him the slightest chance' (12 December 1769). He was not yet fourteen, and had every reason to feel happy: the first ports of call, Rovereto and Verona, were made delightful by the warmth of the Italians' welcome.

So thrilled was Wolfgang by Italy that he translated his second Christian name, Theophilus (Greek for 'beloved of God'), into Italian. He had previously used the German form 'Gottlieb'; now he began to sign himself 'Amadeo' or 'Amadé' – hence the familiar Latin version 'Amadeus'.

Success after success in the towns of Italy

At Mantua the Accademia Filarmonica gave an enthusiastic reception to a recital which consisted of fourteen items without a break, during which Wolfgang sight-read, played the harpsichord and violin, sang, improvised, and included some of his own compositions.

On 23 January 1770 their destination was Milan, where once again they were taken care of by a Salzburger,

Our city cannot but proclaim the remarkable musical abilities of the German boy Wolfgang Amadeus Mozart, who at thirteen is Kapellmeister of the Archbishop of Salzburg. … Last Friday, in a room in the illustrious Accademia Filarmonica and before a large assembly of the nobility of both sexes, this child gave such a display of his skills as to cause utter astonishment.

Gazzetta di Verona
9 January 1770

Count Karl von Firmian, governor of Lombardy and nephew of the Archbishop who had been Leopold's first patron. The carnival season was coming to a climax, with concerts and operas. Piccinni was just putting the finishing touches to his opera *Cesare in Egitto* (*Caesar in Egypt*), which promised to be one of the highlights; Wolfgang and Leopold were allowed to attend the dress rehearsal. They heard works by Luigi Boccherini, made the acquaintance of Giambattista Sammartini, a famous symphony writer who had been Gluck's teacher, and participated in Italian musical life to the full.

A big concert was given on 23 February. Another, some time later, was hosted by Count Firmian, in the presence of 'one hundred and fifty members of the leading nobility'. Both were notable successes. Best of all, Wolfgang was commissioned to write an opera for performance at the end of the year – an *opera seria* or tragedy this time, not an *opera buffa* (comic opera) as for Vienna – in which he would have to follow the strict conventions of form: a somewhat tedious alternation of arias expressing emotions and

The Teatro Ducale, Milan (above), which opened in 1717, saw the first performances of Mozart's *Mithridates* and *Lucio Silla* and of Hasse's *Ruggiero*. It was burnt down in 1776 and replaced by La Scala, which opened two years later. Turin's court theatre was superseded as chief operatic venue in 1741 by the enormous Teatro Regio (opposite, above), which has since been replaced by one yet larger.

recitatives advancing the action. (This was to be *Mithridates*.) Clearly, Milan fell in love with Mozart.

Next stop was the Duchy of Parma, where Mozart was enchanted by the talents of Lucrezia Agujari, known as the 'Bastardella' and renowned for her remarkable singing voice with its extraordinary range. Bologna followed, and here Mozart's one ambition was to be received by the famous Padre Martini.

Padre Martini (1706–84), famous throughout Europe as a scholar and teacher.

Mozart's knowledge of Italian music was limited to the fashionable operas. Padre Martini introduces him to the old masters

Giovanni Battista Martini, now sixty-four, had been the teacher of J. C. Bach, Mozart's London friend. Besides being immensely talented as both a composer and a mathematician, he was the leading authority on all aspects of musical theory. Closeted in the presbytery of San Francesco, from which he seldom emerged, he received Mozart twice and made him work through some arid exercises in counterpoint, to which the young composer submitted with a good grace, showing the venerable priest that despite his youth he was already well versed in the art of fugue.

The relationship was resumed four months later, but meanwhile the Mozarts had an appointment in Florence, which was then a grand-duchy governed by one of Maria Theresa's sons, Leopold. Here further successes awaited them, and here too they met up with old acquaintances, the violinist Pietro Nardini and the castrato Manzuoli. Most unusually, Wolfgang struck up a friendship with someone his own age, the English violinist Thomas Linley, from whom he parted with great reluctance when it was time to go to Rome. They arrived during Holy Week, and Leopold immediately took his son to various religious services, perhaps less out of piety than because this was the best way to meet useful people in their own setting.

In Rome, hearing Allegri's famous *Miserere*, Mozart displays an extraordinary musical memory and maturity

The *Miserere* composed by Gregorio Allegri in the early 16th century was the exclusive property of the Sistine Chapel. Copying it was forbidden; many had tried in vain to note it down. Wolfgang heard it twice and wrote the entire nine-part work out perfectly, on a piece of paper he had hidden in his hat.

The Mozarts liked the Eternal City very much. After a month they moved on to Naples, which disconcerted but soon enchanted them; here, having nothing to gain from King Ferdinand, they enjoyed just seeing the sights. A surprise awaited them on their return to Rome: Pope Clement XIV conferred on Wolfgang the papal knighthood of the Golden Spur. Part of the summer was spent in Bologna, Leopold nursing an injured leg while Wolfgang relaxed with the young Count Pallavicini and made several more visits to Padre Martini, who gave him more and more themes for fugues and corrected his work with endless patience. It was thanks to this

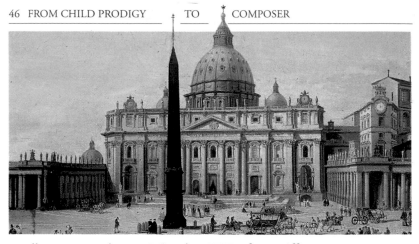

St Peter's Square, Rome.

excellent mentor that on 9 October 1770, after a stiff examination, Mozart was admitted to membership of the prestigious Accademia Filarmonica of Bologna – an exceptional distinction as he was below the requisite age of twenty.

Whereas in Bologna Mozart was an assiduous pupil, in Milan he was already a universally acclaimed composer. Since the start of this journey he

'I only wish that my sister were in Rome, for this town would certainly please her, as St Peter's Church and many other things in Rome are *regular*.'

Wolfgang
14 April 1770

Pope Clement XIV (left) made Mozart a Knight of the Golden Spur, an honour already received by Gluck.

Preceding pages: a painting by the 18th-century Roman artist Giovanni Paolo Pannini, showing a musical entertainment in a fanciful setting.

had only composed a few arias for his castrato friends and an early string quartet (K.80), but now it was time to think about the opera that he had been commissioned to write. He began work in September, starting with the recitatives, deciding to leave the arias until he could judge the competence of the performers. 'God be praised, the first performance of the opera [*Mitridate, rè di Ponto – Mithridates, King of Pontus*] took place on the 26th and won general applause. ... Most unusually for a first night, an aria of the prima donna was encored' (Leopold Mozart, 29 December 1770).

Wolfgang left Milan in high spirits: another opera

Mozart as a Knight of the Golden Spur. This portrait, painted in Salzburg in 1777, also mentions his membership of the musical academies of Bologna and Verona. Its formality is untypical: he is hardly ever known to have worn the insignia.

CAV. AMADEO WOLFGANGO MOZART ACCAD. FILARMON: DI BOLOG. E DI VERONA

had been requested (*Lucio Silla*), Padua had commissioned an oratorio (*La Betulia liberata*, his only excursion into this domain), and Maria Theresa was about to ask him to write a serenade to be played in Milan in 1771 at the wedding of her son, Archduke Ferdinand, to Princess Maria Beatrice d'Este. Arriving home in Salzburg on 28 March, Mozart had every reason to feel satisfied: the future looked full of promise and he knew he would soon be back in his beloved Italy.

In the meantime he resumed his work as Konzertmeister. The days flew by, because he was busy; he fell in love for the first time. He wrote a few religious pieces and four symphonies, and then, on 13 August, it was time to leave. Back to Italy, for four months of concentrated work.

In Milan the wedding festivities began on 15 October. On the 16th, Hasse's opera *Ruggiero* proved a failure, to everyone's surprise. Wolfgang's turn to face first-night nerves came the next day. But he need not have worried; his *Ascanio in Alba* was so well received that it was repeated two days later.

Mozart discovers how unpredictable people in authority can be

Leopold hoped to strike while the iron was hot: why not attempt to obtain a permanent post for his boy in Milan? But his request met with no response from the Archduke. Did Maria Theresa resent Mozart's success, when the opera by Hasse, her former Kapellmeister, had failed? Whatever the reason, her letter to her son (12 December 1771) is uncompromising: 'You ask me to engage the young Salzburger in your service. I do not know why, not believing that you need a composer or useless people of that kind. ... It lowers the tone when such people roam the world like beggars; and furthermore, he has a large family.'

Disappointed, despite the success of *Ascanio*, the Mozarts had to leave Milan with no commissions at all in their pockets.

Their lives are cruelly disrupted: on 16 December 1771 Siegmund von Schrattenbach dies

Von Schrattenbach was succeeded by Count Hieronymus Colloredo. A typical product of the Age of Enlightenment and a close adherent of Joseph II, intelligent, well-informed, but stern and parsimonious, he was disliked and mistrusted by his subjects from the start. Proud of their independence, they were worried about his relationship with the imperial family, and though Colloredo's administrative and cultural reforms may have been appropriate, they were far from popular.

For the time being, though he passed over Leopold in favour of Domenico Fischietti for the post of Kapellmeister, he appreciated Wolfgang's recent compositions (sacred works and church sonatas) and gave him the opportunity to write a theatrical entertainment for his enthronement festivities on 29 April. This was an opera, *Il sogno di Scipione* (*The Dream of Scipio*), to a libretto by Pietro Metastasio (1698-1782).

In October he granted his musicians leave of absence to go to Milan for the premiere of *Lucio Silla*. Nevertheless the Mozarts felt uneasy, as is shown by their use of a code-name when writing about him.

For once Wolfgang was having trouble working. During the summer he had written six symphonies, but a temporary mood of depression is reflected in the arias in *Lucio Silla*. Its successful premiere, on 26 December, was reported by Leopold with less enthusiasm than in the past. A feeler put out to the Grand Duke of Tuscany about possible employment was ignored, and on his return to Salzburg Mozart had nothing more to hope for from Italy.

Opposite: the powerful and popular Maria Theresa, Empress of Austria from 1740 to 1780, Queen of Bohemia and Hungary, received Mozart kindly in 1762 but blocked his progress in 1771.

A cellist, by Watteau. Stringed instruments of the 18th century sounded different from those of today. Steel strings are now more common than gut, producing a tone which is clearer and stronger but less mellow.

Mozart's farewells to Milan were tinged with bitterness; he had so recently been the darling of Italy, yet it proved fickle and made no attempt to detain him. One brief stimulating interlude in Vienna was not enough to dissipate the greyness of his native city, where he had to get used to life as a court musician.

CHAPTER 3

MUSICIAN AND SERVANT

Mozart will always be associated with Salzburg, as he is in this 19th-century image.

But by 1773 it had become for him a provincial city which felt like a prison.

On 13 March 1773 Wolfgang and his father found themselves back home. It is easy to imagine their depressed state of mind, since Leopold had not managed to secure for his son the permanent post he had hoped for – a post which would have been better even than the one he held himself at the court of the Prince-Archbishop.

The ex-prodigy, now seventeen, soon begins to feel suffocated in the narrow confines of his native city

Wolfgang's last Italian journey had been undertaken without great optimism; yet he had composed continually throughout the last months. As well as completing *Lucio Silla* he had added to his collection of string quartets, composing another six (K.155–160), which show a strong Italian influence but are often shot through with a deep melancholy. Some of the slow movements, in poignant minor keys, betray his inner turmoil. Yet the same period saw the composition of the motet *Exsultate, jubilate*, K.165, which ends with a dazzling pyrotechnical display on the word 'Alleluia'. Written for the castrato Venanzio Rauzzini, it is one of Mozart's most popular works today. Wolfgang had always felt unfettered and free to travel, having spent his childhood and adolescence on the move. Now he found himself enclosed in a town he hardly knew, trapped

Salzburg, dominated by its castle, stands beside the river Salzach. In the mid-18th century it was an independent ecclesiastical principality: even the Seven Years War, which broke out in 1756, did not disturb its tranquil routine. Nowadays Salzburg is in Austria, but it was incorporated only in 1816. Mozart, always loyal to his Bavarian origins, liked to think of himself as German.

Left: 'My brother had been quite a good-looking child. But he was disfigured by smallpox, and, what is worse, he came back from Italy with a sallow complexion like an Italian's' (Maria Anna Mozart). Johann Nepomuk della Croce's gouache was probably painted in Salzburg in 1780.

there by the obligations of his employment.
Colloredo had confirmed his appointment as
Konzertmeister, at a salary of 150 florins; he was
therefore under an obligation to be both composer
and performer. Another man might have been happy
with the security this provided, but not Mozart, who
had no desire to live on memories and felt shackled
by the staid, regular rhythm of Salzburg life, which
utterly failed to give him musical satisfaction.
Constantly before his eyes was the example of his
colleague Michael Haydn, misunderstood by an
audience that cared only for the tastes of the moment.
It was hardly to be expected that Mozart should bow
to the demands of his profession if they were going to
conflict with his desires and deflect him from writing
the music he felt deep in his innermost self. Even
Lucio Silla had not conformed to Milanese
expectations of operatic convention.

A post as Kapellmeister at Vienna seems a godsend, but fails to materialize

The ensuing weeks were devoted to
fulfilling commissions from Italy for
wind divertimenti and orchestral
overtures. Meanwhile Leopold had
not given up trying to find his son a
better post. Scarcely had he heard that
Florian Gassmann, Kapellmeister at
Vienna, was seriously ill, than he was
packed and ready to leave.

It was, after all, very tempting. Here
was a reasonable chance of a post as
director of an opera house, for a composer
whose constant dream was of opera. In July
therefore, during the weeks of leave they were
given while the Prince-Archbishop was away taking
the waters, they travelled to the imperial capital. They
were granted an audience with Maria Theresa. 'Her
Majesty the Empress was indeed very gracious to us,
but that was all' (Leopold Mozart, 12 August 1773).

She left them with no illusions. Her attitude had been clear enough in her letter to Ferdinand about 'useless people'.

The congenial atmosphere in Vienna provides Mozart with a new source of inspiration

Despite the financial difficulties which were soon upon him Wolfgang felt carefree. He had met up with his Viennese friends from earlier days, Mesmer and Laugier, the court doctor. And despite the relative lull in cultural activity during the summer months, he was alive to every whiff of the musical ferment that surrounded him and intoxicated his sensibilities. It was the period of the literary *Sturm und Drang* movement (literally, 'storm and stress'), and the writings of F. G. Klopstock, Gotthold Ephraim Lessing and Goethe were finding their echoes in the music of Joseph Haydn and Gluck: emotions driven by intense energy. It was no coincidence that Mozart's burst of symphonic activity in the spring was followed in the late summer by the sudden flowering of the six string quartets K.168–173. Haydn's newest compositions – the famous Op. 20 set of six string quartets – also had their part in this welling-up of inspiration. It seems that Mozart's aesthetic approach now found itself at a parting of the ways, and turned away from

Opposite: Johann Wolfgang von Goethe (1749–1832). He later told his friend Eckermann of seeing Mozart as a child in Frankfurt: 'I saw him as a boy of seven, when he gave a concert when passing through. I myself was about fourteen and I remember still quite clearly the little fellow with his wig and sword.'

• I tell you before God, as an honest man: your son is the greatest composer I know, either in person or by reputation; he has taste and, furthermore, he has the greatest mastery of the art of composition. •
Joseph Haydn to Leopold Mozart, 1785

Mozart and Haydn, depicted in wax.

the Italianate joviality of manner: this increased emotional seriousness is manifest even in the Serenade K.185, written in August in Vienna, perhaps to delight the guests at a wedding, perhaps for students at Salzburg University. But it becomes still more evident after the return to Salzburg in September.

Mozart breaks new ground in the symphony and the piano concerto

The last months of 1773 were marked by renewed creative vigour. First there was a commission from Vienna for incidental music with choir to a play by Tobias Philipp von Gebler, *Thamos, König in Aegypten* (*Thamos, King of Egypt*). It was concerned with the conflict between good and evil, light and dark – eighteen years before *The Magic Flute*. Next came Symphonies nos. 25, K.183, and 28, K.200, in which Mozart's true voice is unmistakable. The former is in his favourite tragic key of G minor and is deeply poignant. No. 28, apparently written a little earlier, is full of astonishing tension. This intense vein, amazing in a composer aged eighteen, continues in the Symphony no. 29, K.201, written in 1774, which marks the definitive break with the earlier so-called symphonies in the Italian tradition, which were merely overtures in three predictable parts.

This change of direction in Mozart's own writing was to influence the history of a whole musical genre.

His originality and determination to turn his back on merely pretty entertainment were confirmed with even more brilliance in his first true piano concerto. (The four preceding ones had been little more than adaptations of pieces by Raupach, Schobert, C. P. E. Bach and others.) This Piano Concerto no. 5, K.175, long remained one of his favourites: he played it again in Vienna in 1782, though with a new finale. Its jaunty swing and jubilant character are apt for a young man overflowing with vitality; the inexhaustible melodic inventiveness, and the treatment of the orchestra as partner rather than

Gala performance at the Teatro Argentina, Rome, 1747, with guests of honour seated on the stage surrounded by musicians on clouds. It was for just such occasions that Mozart's gifts were in demand.

accompaniment, reveal the accomplished master.

The vogue for the concerto grosso, in which a small group of instruments is contrasted with a larger group, had been at its height in the first half of the 18th century. The symphony had ousted it in popularity without, however, impeding the development of the concerto for a single instrument and larger group, which became the soloist's ideal vehicle of expression. Wolfgang's imagination and theatrical sense found in it an inexhaustible source of

inspiration, enriched by influences from many quarters.

The period of exaltation comes to an end and Wolfgang returns to his duties at court

Religious pieces and works for special occasions formed part of his contractual obligations, and he wrote them without reluctance but without enthusiasm. He was back to being a servant, awaiting orders, supplying what was demanded. Such a situation could hardly be expected to satisfy so independent and creative a spirit. Yet with his Symphony no. 30, K.202, dated 5 May 1774, he seemed to accept the situation and even to make concessions to the galant style which was still so fashionable. After all, that was what Colloredo and the Salzburg public demanded, and escape seemed impossible; even Joseph Haydn had to bow to the same situation. Leopold reacted in an unexpected way; years later, on 24 September 1778, he wrote: 'It is better that whatever does you no honour, should not be made public. That is why I have not had any of your symphonies copied, because I know that when you are mature and have more insight, you will be glad that no one has got hold of them, even though at the time you composed them you were pleased enough with them.'

The influence of the pleasing but anodyne galant style is illustrated in the Bassoon Concerto K.191, the Serenade no. 4, K.203, and also to some extent in the first six piano sonatas, K.279–284, which he probably wrote for his own use.

The monotony of his existence is broken by a new commission, this time from the Munich court

The Elector of Bavaria, Maximilian III, wanted a new *opera buffa* for his next carnival season. A libretto by Giuseppe Petrosellini had already been set

On this list of the musicians employed at the Salzburg court in 1775 are the names of Mozart father and son and Michael Haydn.

• Little Wolfgang has no time to write, for he has nothing to do. He is walking up and down the room like a dog with fleas.•

Wolfgang to his sister
8 September 1773

Opposite: Mozart at the spinet.

successfully by Pasquale Anfossi in Rome; but it was quite usual for more than one composer to set the same text.

Still accompanied by his father, Mozart arrived in Munich at the beginning of December 1774, in bitter cold; Nannerl joined them soon afterwards. They were received with great courtesy, and Wolfgang, with his work on *La finta giardiniera* (sometimes known in English as *Sandrina's Secret*) already well advanced, felt perfectly at ease, despite one of the painful gumboils to which he was prone. His letters are full of good humour, abounding with puns, word-play and pseudo-Latin quotations.

The premiere of the opera was arranged for 29 December, but by the 20th rehearsals had hardly begun.

The success of *La finta giardiniera* on 13 January is such that, once again, all seems possible

The Mozarts began to hope for a commission for an *opera seria*, which was more prestigious for a composer than *opera buffa*; all the more so because Wolfgang's recent success had eclipsed Antonio Tozzi's *Orfeo*, billed as the climax of the carnival. 'Thank God! My opera was performed yesterday, the 13th, for the first time and was such a success that I cannot describe the applause to Mamma. . . . Our return to Salzburg will not happen very soon, and Mamma should not wish it. . . . Mamma knows how good it is for me to be able to breathe freely. We shall come back soon

enough' (Wolfgang, 14 January 1775).

As for Colloredo, he passed through Munich during January and heard the praise being lavished on his Konzertmeister without paying much attention. Had Leopold been exaggerating its warmth? Anyway, the more cautious critics were always careful to leave a question mark over the future of the former infant prodigy; thus C. F. D. Schubart in the *Deutsche Chronik*: 'I have just heard an *opera buffa* by the admirably gifted Mozart. Provided he has not reached his peak too early, Mozart will become one of the finest composers of all time.' Meanwhile Wolfgang enjoyed the easy agreeable life of Munich, where it was so not to be treated like a servant; Count Seeau,

• I went to the theatre yesterday to see the comedy "Mode nach der Haushaltung" ["The Fashionable Household"], which was very well acted. ...
Your Munich brother, the 1774th day of Anno 30, Dicembre. •
Wolfgang to his sister

• Wolfgang's opera went down so well at the first rehearsal that the performance has been postponed until 5 January to give the singers the chance to learn it better. ...
The composition of the music met with surprisingly great approval. ... Now it all depends on the production in the theatre, and we hope that all will go well, for the actors are not ill-disposed towards us. •
Leopold Mozart
28 December 1774

Left: Munich, with the tower of St Peter's Church.

who was in charge of musical and visual entertainment, received him with deference.

It was thus hardly surprising that Mozart's stay was prolonged while *La finta giardiniera* received several more performances and two of his masses were heard in the court chapel. Perhaps to test the young man's professionalism as well as his talent, the Elector expressed a desire for a motet in counterpoint. Mozart responded with his offertory *Misericordias Domini*, K.222.

Munich lets Mozart leave empty-handed

Mozart left Munich with no guarantee that he would be offered any post that might become vacant. His only commission was an unofficial one: the music-loving Baron Thaddeus von Dürnitz requested keyboard sonatas and bassoon pieces. Mozart took part in a friendly contest, such as were then fashionable, on the harpsichord with the gifted Captain Notger von Beecke. Then the family departed, arriving back in Salzburg on 7 March 1775. Mozart would have been surprised and disappointed if he had known that this time he would be staying for thirty months.

However, all went well to begin with. The Prince-Archbishop asked his Konzertmeister to compose a theatrical entertainment for Archduke Maximilian Franz, visiting Salzburg on his way back from seeing

The violin is the ideal virtuoso instrument and also the one with the greatest 'singing' powers. Whenever Mozart wrote for the violin he seemed to be thinking of the human voice and its incomparable expressive qualities.

Before 1775, the only concertos Wolfgang had written were small ones for insertion into serenades and cassations. Now he finally gave the violin full-scale works to play.

his sister Marie Antoinette at Versailles. This was the enchanting *Il rè pastore* (*The Shepherd King*), to a libretto by the indefatigable Metastasio. But once that excitement had died down, Mozart was back to the old routine. His professional duties included playing the violin, as Colloredo was quick to remind him. Between April and December 1775 he produced five violin concertos of which two – No. 3, K.216, and No. 5, K.219 – show the composer triumphing over the limitations of the galant style and preserving his originality. The concertos testify to his talents as a violinist and also illustrate the various stages of the genre as it underwent rapid development at the time.

1776: Mozart, now twenty, has no more to hope for from life in the provinces

His existence in Salzburg seemed to be leading nowhere. Routine was tedious, and to make matters worse Colloredo closed the court theatre. Once more the story of Mozart's life can be traced in the list of works composed: masses, divertimenti, occasional pieces for local aristocrats. These included the *Serenata notturna* K.239 for two small orchestras, the Piano Concerto no. 7 for three pianos, K.242, written for the Countess of Lodron and her two daughters, and the Piano Concerto no. 8, K.246, intended for another pupil, Countess von Lützow – all works of supreme distinction, in which the hand of Mozart is unmistakable from the first bars. But a more ambitious work was the Serenade in D, K.250, the *Haffner*, written for the wedding of Marie Elisabeth Haffner, daughter of an eminent Salzburg businessman.

Archbishop Colloredo of Salzburg. The Mozarts referred to him as 'the Mufti'.

Strangely enough, the latter part of the year was devoted to religious music, as if Mozart were putting his early life behind him and beginning to question everything. He turned for counsel to Padre Martini, sending him the motet he had written in Munich and asking for his opinion. 'Most reverend Padre Maestro, my esteemed Patron, the regard, the esteem and respect which I cherish for your illustrious person have prompted me to trouble you with this letter and to send you a humble specimen of my music, which I submit to your masterly judgment. ... I live in a country where music has a struggle to exist. ... The situation regarding the theatre is bad because of a lack of singers. ... I amuse myself by writing chamber music and music for the church, in which branches of composition we have two other excellent masters of counterpoint, Signori Haydn and Adlgasser.' The scholar's reply was courteous if a little formal, like an academic tutor's report. 'I found the motet very pleasing...for it contains all the elements that modern music requires. ... I trust that you will continue to apply yourself unremittingly, for, by its very nature, music demands much study and practice throughout one's life.'

Mozart reaches an irrevocable decision: to leave Salzburg

Leopold had in mind another concert tour, with the ultimate aim of finding his son a better post. But he reckoned without Colloredo, who ignored the request for leave, using as a pretext the imminent visit of Joseph II, who would shortly be passing through the city: all members of his court band were required to be present. A third application met with a third rebuff to Leopold; but his son would be allowed to be absent if he wished.

Since the beginning of 1777 Wolfgang had produced just one significant work, the Piano Concerto no. 9, K.271. Its opening bars resound like an independence march, and it constitutes the first in a long series of piano concertos in which his genius

flowered as nowhere else except in his operas. Mozart's meeting with its dedicatee, the French pianist Mademoiselle Jeunehomme, and with the singer Josepha Duschek some time later, were two bright interludes in an otherwise dark period.

For though Colloredo took less and less notice of his Konzertmeister, other than to use him as a concert performer, he was still reluctant to let him leave. Finally Wolfgang could bear it no longer. On 1 August 1777 he resigned his post. The Archbishop's response was swift. On 28 August it was decreed that both father and son were free to seek their fortune elsewhere. The prospect of financial insecurity alarmed Leopold, who was beginning to feel his age; he gave in and decided to stay. But on 23 September Wolfgang, with his mother, bade Salzburg farewell.

Mozart could breathe again. He had struggled free of the pressures, the boredom and the tyrannical restrictions imposed by those who desired to control what music he wrote, and he had shaken the dust of Salzburg off his feet. His pulse quickening with hope, he set off for Munich, sure that his genius was about to be acknowledged by the world at large. He was twenty-one – still young enough to have illusions…

CHAPTER 4

DISILLUSIONMENT

'I am always in my best humour, for my heart has been as light as a feather ever since I got away from all that petty scheming!'

Wolfgang
26 September 1777

23 September 1777 was a sad day for Leopold Mozart. He was left at home in Salzburg with the watchful Nannerl while his wife and son departed for a prolonged absence. 'After you had both left, I walked up our stairs very wearily and threw myself down in a chair. When we said good-bye, I had made great efforts to control myself in order not to make our parting more painful. ... I was astonished how Nannerl wept, and I had the greatest difficulty in consoling her. ... We played piquet and then had supper in my room and, ... with God's blessing, went to bed. That is how we spent the sad day which I never thought I should have to face' (Leopold Mozart, 25 September 1777). But Wolfgang was in such high spirits that it was useless to attempt to conceal his delight at getting away from 'the Mufti' (Colloredo) – so much so that Leopold had to caution him: 'My dear Wolfgang, I beg you not to write any more jokes about our Mufti. Remember that I am in Salzburg and that one of your letters might get lost or find its way into the wrong hands.'

Above: 'Allerliebster Papa!', Wolfgang's greeting to his 'dearest papa' in a letter of 1777. In that year Leopold Mozart (right) was fifty-eight. His career was more or less over. He would spend his remaining years in Salzburg, never quite realizing his aspirations. As a crowning irony, his *Toy* Symphony, his most enduringly popular work, was long attributed to Joseph Haydn.

By 24 September the travellers had reached Munich. Fortified by his reputation and the success three years earlier of *La finta giardiniera*, Mozart renewed his contact with Count Seeau and also sought out the Bishop of Chiemsee, Prince von Zeil, who was in charge of the theatres. He even had the opportunity of meeting the Elector Maximilian III in person, thanks to the cellist Franz Xaver Woschitka, who arranged a supposedly chance encounter.

Munich from the west. Left of centre, the domed Theatine Church; right, the twin-towered Frauenkirche.

Mozart learns a hard lesson: never antagonize a prince

It was all in vain. Word that he had been dissatisfied

⁕Dearest Papa, I cannot write in verse, for I am no poet. I cannot arrange words and phrases artistically so as to produce effects of light and shade, for I am no painter. Even by signs and gestures I cannot express my thoughts and feelings, for I am no dancer. But I can do so through sounds, for I am a composer.⁕

Wolfgang
8 November 1777

with his former patron had already reached the ears of Maximilian; etiquette forbade that the Elector should take the side of a servant, and he had no wish to quarrel with an influential neighbour. Wolfgang drew the ruler's attention again to his credentials, but Maximilian knew them perfectly well already: it was in fact he who had sent Wolfgang the message, via Zeil, that he should go and make his name in Italy before looking for any permanent post.

Mozart was naïve. Leopold, so experienced in the ways of the court, proffered advice, but his son refused to think about who or what might be useful to him and advance his cause. Some of his friends,

Mozart's exquisite lightness of touch is the result of a perfect balance between brilliant inventiveness and disciplined expression. He was totally free of the clichéd superficiality of some 18th-century art, of which Fragonard's *The Swing* may be seen as typical. His delightful creations are never without a shadow of melancholy.

such as Franz Joseph Albert, an innkeeper and an enthusiastic organizer of concerts, would have liked to keep him in Munich: Albert was even prepared to pay him an allowance until he obtained employment – an offer which wounded Leopold's paternal pride. Another idea of Wolfgang's was to contribute to the rebirth of German opera, in a country currently saturated with Italian. But he did nothing decisive. At the city hospital he ran into the composer Joseph Mysliveček, whom he had met in Bologna in 1770, who tried to persuade him to return to Italy. Finally Leopold wrote sternly from Salzburg to bring him to his senses, and he obeyed: he continued his journey to Mannheim, stopping off at Augsburg.

Sau

Porco

Cochon

Sus

Wolfgang's cousin Maria Anna Thekla Mozart, nicknamed 'the Bäsle'. In one of his joky letters to her, an ink blot is surrounded by the word for 'pig' in four languages.

The staid city of Augsburg quickly discourages the temperamental Wolfgang

Augsburg was where Leopold Mozart's family came from, but it had little to offer Wolfgang. A free city, it was populated by well-to-do, long-established citizens, and even its musicians were people of a certain social standing, such as Friedrich Graf, a local composer whose words were 'all on stilts' (letter of 14 October 1777). Wolfgang's malicious pen had a field day. He found an unexpected ally in his cousin Maria Anna Thekla, 'the Bäsle', daughter of his bookbinder uncle. She was no prude; it was to her that he addressed some of his crudest letters, whose unsubtle scatological humour has deeply troubled his more fastidious admirers and puzzled scholars ever since.

•On the morning of this day, the 17th, I write and declare that our little cousin is beautiful, intelligent, charming, clever and gay; and that is because she has mixed with people a great deal, and has also spent some time in Munich. … Indeed we two get on extremely well, for, like myself, she is slightly wicked. We make fun of everyone together and laugh a lot.•

Wolfgang
17 October 1777

At Augsburg he had another meeting with Johann Andreas Stein, the eminent piano manufacturer whose pianos and organs he had so admired on a previous visit in 1763. The hours of delight spent at the console in St Ulrich's Church obliterated from his mind the ponderous smugness of the rich merchants who had been the butt of his irony, and he found himself agreeing to appear at an 'Akademie' on 22 October. At the last moment he almost refused to go on because the mayor's son stupidly made fun of the Golden Spur insignia which, on Leopold's insistent advice, he had put on for the occasion. To add insult to injury, the concert was poorly attended. Memories of his lukewarm reception in Augsburg in 1763 were revived, and he left as soon as he could.

Philippe Mercier, *A Music Party*. The word 'academy' means in modern English a learned institution or an educational or training establishment. In Mozart's Germany the term *Akademie* was used for societies which organized concerts and, by extension, the concerts themselves.

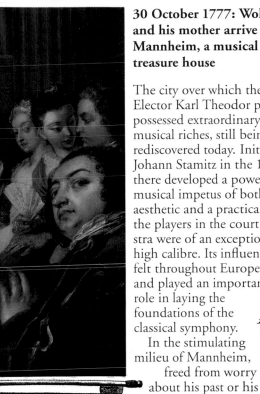

30 October 1777: Wolfgang and his mother arrive in Mannheim, a musical treasure house

The city over which the Elector Karl Theodor presided possessed extraordinary musical riches, still being rediscovered today. Initiated by Johann Stamitz in the 1740s, there developed a powerful musical impetus of both an aesthetic and a practical kind: the players in the court orchestra were of an exceptionally high calibre. Its influence was felt throughout Europe and played an important role in laying the foundations of the classical symphony.

In the stimulating milieu of Mannheim, freed from worry about his past or his reputation, Wolfgang experienced a rebirth. His genius was finally recognized by some of the foremost musicians: the composers Johann Christian Cannabich and Ignaz Holzbauer, the flautist Johann Baptist Wendling and his family, the oboist Friedrich Ramm, the violinist Christian Danner, the tenor Anton Raaff. All gave him friendship and guidance which was both competent and much appreciated. He paid little heed to the antagonism of Abbé Vogler, the court Kapellmeister, or Johann Sterkel, a

Karl Theodor (1724-99), Elector Palatine and then Elector of Bavaria, a passionate patron of the arts and sciences. He had close ties with Voltaire as well as with leading German men of letters. In 1775 he founded the German Palatine Society for the defence of German language and literature.

minor composer, both of whom found him too impetuous, nor to the exhortations of Leopold, who was alarmed to see his son frequenting the company of people of unconventional morality.

Karl Theodor, whose reign in the Palatinate had begun in 1749, was an ardent patron of the arts and sciences. He had been much influenced by French fashions, and sought at his court to emulate Versailles, but then he decided to champion a return to a national culture. The 'German national theatre' which he had just founded was inexpressibly exciting for Wolfgang. Their encounter on 6 November after a concert was cordial enough for Mozart to hope he might be asked for a new opera.

But the days passed and no message came from the court. Money began to run out, Leopold became anxious, and there was a voluminous exchange of letters. Leopold's become agitated: 'Not a word about where you are going or what plans you may be making. ... The object of your journey...was and is and must be to obtain an appointment or to earn some money. ... You, however, seem to think nothing matters' (27 November 1777).

Karl Theodor's reply finally came, and it was negative. But Mozart stayed on in Mannheim. He felt so at home there and was so happily composing that he simply ignored his money problems. The death of the Elector of Bavaria, Maximilian III, came as a jolt: Karl Theodor succeeded him and moved to Munich, soon followed by his entourage.

In January 1778 a lucky chance presented itself during a brief visit to the Princess of Orange at Kirchheim-Bolanden. Wolfgang wrote to his father on 17 January: 'I shall get eight louis d'or at least, for, since she is extremely fond of singing, I have had four arias copied for her; and, since she has a nice little orchestra and gives a concert every day, I shall also present her with a symphony. The copying of the arias will not cost me much, for it has been done by a certain Herr Weber, who will go there with me. I

DER RHEIN

Aloysia Weber was a coloratura soprano. The concert aria *Popoli di Tessaglia* (*People of Thessaly*), which Mozart wrote for her, goes up to G above high C.

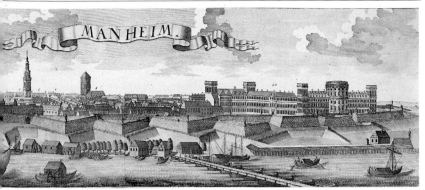

don't know whether I have already written about his daughter or not – she sings really most admirably…'

Wolfgang has just turned twenty-two; Aloysia is only eighteen…

Wolfgang had fallen madly in love with the young singer. He desired more and more to write an opera, an Italian one which would draw attention to his beloved. He was quite incapable of withholding from his father the news of his dawning passion and his hopes for the future. Leopold was aghast. Fridolin Weber was only a lowly copyist and member of the chorus at the court theatre: to Leopold, who minded about respectability and cherished social ambitions for his son, a match with Aloysia Weber seemed disastrous.

Would Wolfgang give in to his father's persuasions and his obvious distress? Leopold resorted to emotional blackmail, pointing out that he was getting old, that Nannerl was sacrificing her own career giving lessons in order to finance the household, and that Wolfgang's travels were simply getting the family into debt.

It seems that Wolfgang did pay heed, though without giving up his love or his creative ambitions. He consented to go to Paris, after presenting his friends (Raaff and the Wendlings) and Aloysia with several more arias and ariettas.

Mannheim in the early 18th century; the vast electoral palace is at the right. It was during the reign of Karl Philipp, father of Karl Theodor, that Mannheim made a determined effort to emancipate itself from the influence of Italy and become a musical centre in its own right. Then between 1745 and 1777 its complement of singers and instrumentalists virtually doubled. The Mannheim musicians were fine players and often composers too. They excelled in performing *sinfonie concertanti* (in which a group of solo instruments is set off against a larger orchestra), the genre which they made their particular speciality.

Wolfgang and his mother set off for Paris. The journey took nine and a half days. 'We really thought that we should not be able to endure it,' wrote Wolfgang on 23 March 1778, 'for never in my life have I been so bored.' Anna Maria was dejected. She missed Salzburg, and sensed that her son put up with her presence rather than being glad of it. She was apprehensive of finding herself in a foreign country of whose language she knew not a word. As for Mozart, he was meditating on the advice offered by Baron Grimm in response to an appeal from Leopold.

Wolfgang is forced to take pupils in order to survive in Paris

Wolfgang had already eloquently expressed what he felt about giving lessons: 'I will gladly give lessons as

Fragonard, *The Music Lesson*. It is hard to imagine Mozart teaching. In his correspondence he admits to an aversion for an occupation he considered unbearably boring unless the pupil was really gifted; but worse than that, he felt that it should be left to those who could do nothing else: he realized that he was a genius, that genius could not be taught, and that time was too precious to waste.

a favour, especially when I see that my pupil has talent, inclination and a desire to learn; but to be forced to go to a house at a particular hour, or to have to wait at home for a pupil – that is something I cannot do, no matter how much money I might earn. ... I neither can nor should bury in this way the talent for composition with which God in his goodness has so richly endowed me' (letter of 7 February 1778). But now he had no choice.

The first days were disagreeable, in a sordid lodging where it was impossible even to bring a keyboard instrument up the stairs. But Baron Grimm and his friend, Madame d'Epinay, undertook to introduce the young man into some good houses; and some of his Mannheim friends – Wendling, Ramm and Raaff – were there too.

Soon Anna Maria's letters to her husband took on a more positive tone. They had found decent lodgings, and Wolfgang had been able to meet Jean Le Gros, director of the Concerts Spirituels, and renew acquaintance with Georges Noverre, Director of Ballet at the Opéra. He had also been presented to the Comte de Guines, who was in favour at court; Mozart wrote the famous Concerto for Flute and Harp K.299 for the duke and his daughter, who was one of his pupils.

These moments of satisfaction had to compensate for certain others which were just the reverse, such as

A quartet formed by a tiny *violino piccolo*, harp, flute and horn: painting by Pierre Antoine Baudouin (1723-69).

The harp in use in Mozart's time was not the modern concert harp, which was perfected by Sebastien Erard in the early 19th century. Around 1720 a series of developments had produced the pedal harp of Georg Hochbrucker. The instrument had seven pedals, each corresponding to a note of the scale. This is the kind of harp for which Mozart wrote the concerto K.299 in which the harp's crystalline notes are joined by an ideal partner, the flute. The concerto makes concessions to the galant style in vogue at the time in France, but Mozart's poetry shines through.

the occasion when he was invited to the Duchesse de Chabot, treated with a politeness akin to extreme disdain, kept waiting in an icy-cold room, and then made to play on a bad piano while the assembled company occupied itself sketching.

There were other disappointments. The parts of the Sinfonia Concertante K.297b, which was to be premiered at a Concert Spirituel by Wendling and his companions, playing flute, oboe, bassoon and horn, were not even copied out for the performers. Wolfgang suspected Giuseppe Maria Cambini (a composer now forgotten), who feared a challenge to his supremacy; the real cause was probably negligence on the part of Le Gros. Whatever the reason, it was a pity for this luxuriant work in which French taste was supplanted by the spirit of Mannheim.

In the midst of all these contretemps, whose influence may be traced in anguished moments in the Piano Sonata no. 8, K.310, Le Gros commissioned a symphony, probably to make amends. The Symphony no. 31, K.297, the *Paris*, performed on 18 June at the Concert Spirituel, is like a burst of sunshine.

But Paris turned its back on Mozart. All he was offered was a post of organist at Versailles, which he did not want. He

Flute and bassoon, from Diderot and d'Alembert's *Encyclopaedia*. The Sinfonia Concertante K.297b was intended for flute, oboe, bassoon and horn. The only surviving copy specifies instead of the flute the clarinet – a new instrument, which Mozart loved. He hated the flute, and claimed that writing for instruments he hated made him numb.

detested the French capital, finding it too capricious and subject to the whims of fashion.

Tragedy strikes

In the middle of June Anna Maria's delicate health began to decline; she was struck down by a fever, fell into a coma, and died peacefully on 3 July. Wolfgang's grief and sense of isolation were profound, though his sense of propriety led him to conceal them beneath a mask of resignation. But at the same time, freed from a parental vigilance which had started to oppress him, he began to feel more enterprising. Although Aloysia was still present in his thoughts, he considered extending his stay in Paris in the hope of obtaining a commission for an opera.

The church and cemetery of the Holy Innocents in Paris, where Mozart's mother's funeral took place. 'By the mercy of God I have borne it all with fortitude and composure. When her illness became dangerous I prayed to God for two things only – a happy death for her, and strength and courage for myself' (Wolfgang, letter of 3 July 1778).

But he reckoned without Leopold and Grimm: they had continued to correspond, and Leopold accepted everything the baron said without question. Wolfgang had had to borrow money from his patron and was reminded in no uncertain terms of his debt; furthermore, he had offended him by refusing to side with the supporters of Piccinni against Gluck in a Parisian musical feud.

Wolfgang was somewhat consoled at the beginning of August by a visit from Johann Christian Bach and the castrato Tenducci. But his father was putting increased pressure on him in a final bid to get him to return to Germany, renewing his entreaties to Karl Theodor, appealing to Padre Martini to help. The Salzburg organist Adlgasser and Kapellmeister Lolli had died; now was his chance. Colloredo agreed and even guaranteed that he would allow Wolfgang leave of absence to honour any contracts or commissions he might be offered. If he refused now, he might be the death of his father and would inherit all his debts. If he accepted, Aloysia could come to Salzburg too and try her luck at court.

Full of dread, Mozart reluctantly agrees to return to Salzburg

On 26 September Grimm arranged for a carriage to take Wolfgang to Strasbourg, where he was to give three concerts. On 29 September he arrived – in Mannheim, on an unexpected detour to Aloysia's home town. Leopold was furious. Aloysia herself had just been offered a position in Munich; Mozart followed her there, and the longed-for reunion took place on Christmas Day. But when he had last seen her she had been a young singer just starting out, whereas now she was an established soprano, whose only thought was her career. Mozart received a cruel rebuff. His parting gift to her, however, the concert aria *Popoli di Tessaglia* (*People of Thessaly*), was splendid – an ideal vehicle to display her voice to the best possible advantage.

Nannerl, Wolfgang and Leopold Mozart in 1781, with the dead Anna Maria present in the form of her portrait.

After presenting the Electress with the Violin Sonatas K.301–306, engraved in Paris, there was nothing for Mozart to do but continue his return journey, accompanied by his good friend and cousin 'the Bäsle'. On 16 January 1779, after a separation of fifteen months, Wolfgang was reunited with his father and sister in Salzburg. But it was a melancholy occasion, for Anna Maria Mozart lay buried in France.

If your mother had come back home from Mannheim, she would not have died. … You would have got to Paris at a better time…and my poor wife would still be [alive] in Salzburg.
Leopold Mozart
27 August 1778

Mozart had given up the struggle and resigned himself to suffering the obnoxious Colloredo again. But his creative stock had been enriched by his contacts with Italian, German and French music; and now he knew, even if the public still did not, that he was an unrivalled genius.

CHAPTER 5
'MY HAPPINESS IS
JUST BEGINNING'

In the later 19th century, Mozart was seen as the inspired musician (opposite).

On 17 January 1779, just ten days before his twenty-third birthday, Mozart took up his post as official organist to the Prince-Archbishop of Salzburg. His return had been sad, everyday routine was tedious, and he disliked being obliged to supply works to order (though one of these, in March, was the *Coronation Mass*); but a diversion appeared in the form of a travelling theatrical company directed by a certain Boehm. Opera was once again to the fore. For this company he made *La finta giardiniera* into a *Singspiel*, the German type of comic opera in which arias alternate with spoken dialogue. Another singspiel, *Zaïde ou le Sérail* (*Zaide, or the Seraglio*), remained unfinished, but a few months later he started work on *Die Entführung aus dem Serail* (*The Abduction from the Seraglio*, usually known as *The Seraglio*). Boehm's actors were followed by another troupe, led by Emanuel Schikaneder, future librettist of *The Magic Flute*.

Mozart, desperately bored, almost loses the will to compose

Theatre broke the monotony, as he discovered the works of Shakespeare and two contemporary playwrights – the Frenchman Pierre Antoine Caron de Beaumarchais and the German Lessing; and Leopold seemed happy to have him around.

But Mozart wrote little. Amongst his better works at this time were the Symphony no. 33, K.319 (only his second symphony since 1774) and the unique Serenade K.230, featuring the merry calls of the posthorn which give it its nickname, but containing moments of pathos too. Best of all was the Sinfonia Concertante for Violin and Viola K.364, a grandiose work of extraordinary expressive power. But the next months saw virtually no compositions: his next work, the Symphony no. 34, K.338, is dated 29 August. Either he had a temporary block or he was declining to compose in the genres demanded by his job or by the tastes of the Salzburg public.

The second half of the 18th century saw the height of the vogue for concertos and *sinfonie concertanti*; both offered opportunities for felicitous combinations of contrasting instruments. Keyboard and violin were especially favoured, but the oboe, trumpet and clarinet were also popular. For the horn Mozart wrote four concertos, all dedicated to his friend Ignaz Leutgeb, horn-player

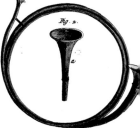

and cheesemonger. The horn's solemn yet warm tone is a favourite with audiences, although it is perhaps the most difficult of all instruments to master, especially in its upper register. In this group portrait of instruments (opposite) horns share a sort of cosy domesticity with violin, recorder and cello.

The violin

An imaginary 18th-century workshop illustrating musical instruments, chiefly strings. Until the Renaissance, musicians made their own instruments. The violin as we know it was perfected in Italy during the 17th and 18th centuries by Amati and his pupils Stradivari and Guarneri in Cremona and also by Bertolotti and Maggini in Brescia. Earlier stringed instruments were the viols, held on or between the legs (hence the term 'viola da gamba'), and the fiddles, held on the arm, used to accompany folk-dancing. The violin gained supremacy at the end of the 17th century as one of the most prestigious solo instruments.

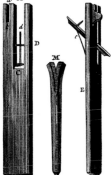

Keyboard instruments

Square or table piano
(above left), harp-
sichord (below left) and
spinet (below right). In
the harpsichord and
spinet each string is
plucked by a leather or
quill plectrum attached
to a pivoted tongue in a
jack (above). The
harpsichord strongly
influenced the
development of musical
form in Europe. The
spinet is smaller and
quieter and its strings
often run diagonally to
the keyboard. Both were
superseded by the piano,
developed in the 18th
century. There, because
the strings are struck
rather than plucked,
volume could be subtly
varied and two new
possibilities arose: the
melody could be
brought out in relation
to the accompaniment,
and passages could grow
gradually louder or
softer. Notes could also
be sustained for a longer
time.

IDOMENEO.
DRAMMA
PER
MUSICA
DA RAPPRESENTARSI
NEL TEATRO NUOVO DI
CORTE
PER COMANDO
DI S. A. S. E.
CARLO TEODORO
Come Palatino del Rheno, Duca dell'
alta, e bassa Baviera, e del Palatinato
Superiore, etc. etc. Archidapifero,
et Elettore, etc. etc.
NEL CARNOVALE
1781.

La Poesia è del Signor Abate Giambattista Varesco
Capellano di Corte di S. A. R. l'Arcivescovo, e Principe di Salisburgo.
La Musica è del Signor Maestro Wolfgango Amadeo Mozart Academico di Bologna, e di Verona, in
fin attual servizio di S. A. R. l'Arcivescovo, e Principe
di Salisburgo.
La Traduzione è del Signor Andrea Schachtner,
pure in attual servizio di S. A. R. l'Arcivescovo, e
Principe di Salisburgo.

MONACO,
Appresso Francesco Giuseppe Thuille.

At last, the chance to write a full-scale grand opera, *Idomeneo*

Karl Theodor, now installed in Munich as Elector of Bavaria, ordered an *opera seria* for the carnival. The libretto of *Idomeneo, rè di Creta* (*Idomeneo, King of Crete*) bore the signature of the Salzburg court chaplain, G. B. Varesco. Colloredo, unable to resist this double honour, granted his organist leave of absence.

The Weber family had left Munich to be with Aloysia, who was now in Vienna, but Mozart's old friends Wendling, Raaff, Cannabich and the flautist Becke were there. Mozart, surrounded by affection, responded with a particularly frenzied burst of creative activity: 'My head and my hands are so full of Act III that it would be no wonder if I were to turn into a third act myself' (letter of 3 January 1781).

When the Empress Maria Theresa died, Colloredo had to go to Vienna. Leopold and Nannerl took advantage of his absence to go to the premiere of *Idomeneo* on 29 January 1781. It was a triumph, but a short-lived one. People found the music baffling: it broke the rigid conventions of *opera seria* by giving real emotions and individuality to the protagonists. But Mozart was happy.

Colloredo, however, ordered him to come to Vienna. Their relationship degenerated into open hostility. Flushed by his recent success, Mozart would no

The genre of *opera seria* reached its peak in the 18th century. In the librettos by Metastasio and others the action was moved on by recitatives and halted by arias expressing the emotions of the characters, usually heroes from mythology or classical antiquity. Much emphasis was laid on moral virtues in these highly artificial and formal texts. In a painting from the school of Pietro Longhi (opposite) we see a typical scene in a Venetian opera house.

longer tolerate being treated like a servant; and he had after all made some headway in Viennese aristocratic circles. It irked him to be reduced to the same level as other employees of the Archbishop, such as the violinist Antonio Brunetti and the castrato Francesco Ceccarelli.

Animosity begins to boil over, to Mozart's secret delight

Colloredo's motives are inscrutable. Perhaps he felt that his rebellious employee's presence upset the rest of the court orchestra by setting higher standards than theirs, and he wanted to keep him in his place. Certainly he provoked Wolfgang's hostility by attempting (in vain) to prevent him from taking part in a charity concert organized by the Vienna Musicians' Society for the benefit of the widows and orphans of musicians.

• I have here [in Vienna] the finest and most useful acquaintances in the world. ... All possible honour is shown me and I am paid into the bargain. So why expect me to languish in Salzburg for the sake of 400 gulden, hanging about being no use to anyone, being neither properly paid nor encouraged? ... What would be the end of it? I'll tell you. I should have to endure worse and worse insults, or go away again.•
Wolfgang to Leopold
12 May 1781

Mozart had realized that it would be in his interest to stay in Vienna. His recent success, his relationships with members of the aristocracy, including Countess Thun and Count Cobenzl, the presence of good friends such as Dr Mesmer: everything led him to believe that he would be able to earn his living in the capital, especially as the Inspector of the German National Theatre, Gottlieb Stephanie the younger, was thinking of asking him for an opera. So he waited for the rupture; he even longed for it, to Leopold's alarm. It came soon enough. In Wolfgang's partly coded letter of 9 May to his father he relates in detail the stormy interview which led to his dismissal, sparing no detail of the abuse which the archbishop, beside himself with rage, heaped on him. His letter ends: 'Now please be cheerful, for my happiness is just beginning, and I trust that my happiness will be yours also. … I want nothing more to do with Salzburg.' Was this the first time in musical history that a composer put his art above all else, refused the security of servitude and opted for liberty?

It took another month to be sure of his independence, for Leopold attempted to intervene, asking Count Arco for assistance. The Count lectured the defiant Wolfgang on how to behave: he was later to be proved right on some points, as for instance when he warned him against the inconstancy and frivolity of the Viennese. He finished his diatribe, as is well known, by kicking the young man out of the room. Mozart turned his back on Salzburg and settled down in Vienna.

The Domgasse, Vienna, where Mozart composed *The Marriage of Figaro*.

• You must be patient for a little while longer and then I shall be able to prove to you how useful Vienna is going to be to us all. … When I am in Salzburg I long for a hundred amusements, but here not for a single one. For just to be in Vienna is in itself entertainment enough. •
Wolfgang to Leopold
26 May 1781

Independence does not come cheap: Mozart finds himself penniless in Vienna

Starting in May he lodged at the Webers'. Aloysia was now married, to Josef Lange, and his thoughts had not yet turned to her sister Constanze; he was just a lodger like anyone else. Little by little life began to get organized. He took one pupil, Countess Rumbeke, and launched a subscription for the publication (by Artaria) of four violin sonatas, K.376, 377, 379 and 380. But it was summertime and musical activity was limited. The theatre threw him a lifeline: Gottlieb Stephanie confirmed the commission for *The Seraglio* and sent him the libretto.

At last Wolfgang was about to write a German opera and thus participate in the revival of the national art desired by Joseph II. It took a year to turn the dream into reality, and meanwhile his relationship with Leopold was strained almost to breaking point.

Constanze Weber enters the scene

Gossip travels fast, and Leopold soon heard that Wolfgang was interested in Aloysia's younger sister. A warm affection had sprung up between Wolfgang and Constanze, though he was not really in love with her as he had been with Aloysia. Pressurized by Johann Thorwart, the Weber girls' guardian since the death of their father, and by their mother, Wolfgang agreed to the engagement, partly to save Constanze from an unhappy home. He justified his decision to his father in a letter of

Left: Antonio Salieri (1750-1825), appointed court composer in Vienna in 1774, was a predecessor rather than a serious rival, though his scheming against *Così fan tutte* in 1790 was a worry for Mozart.

Opposite: Mozart playing before Joseph II at Schönbrunn, as imagined in a 19th-century engraving. The Emperor is unlikely to have listened with such respectful concentration.

Mozart and Catarina Cavalieri. He wrote Constanze in the *Seraglio* for her and added the aria 'Mi tradì' when she sang Elvira in the Vienna premiere of *Don Giovanni*.

15 December 1781: 'She is not witty, but she has enough sound common sense to be able to fulfil her duties as a wife and mother.'

The Seraglio was not progressing and he was not composing much else either. He still hoped for a position at court, for instance as tutor to Elisabeth of Württemberg, but he was passed over in favour of Antonio Salieri. Soon, however, a piano contest with Muzio Clementi, in which he was able to outshine the famous composer and virtuoso, enhanced his reputation and gave him new optimism. Amongst his pupils were Frau von Trattner, wife of a rich publisher, and Countesses Pálffy and Zichy: the income from their lessons was enough to live on. But Leopold continued to write bitterly reproachful letters, which the prospect of the marriage did nothing to improve. Yet Wolfgang still wished sincerely for his father's blessing.

In 1782 all practicalities are forgotten as Mozart discovers J. S. Bach

The big event in his musical life at this time came when Baron Gottfried van Swieten introduced him to the works of Handel and particularly Johann Sebastian Bach. Bach's son Johann Christian, his friend, had just died. Mozart was so enraptured by the beauty and complexity of the father's works that he transcribed fugues from the *Well-tempered Clavier* for the baron's orchestra and also improvised some preludes.

During the summer he was involved in a series of Sunday open-air concerts held at the Augarten and in some of Vienna's

‖ This piece [*The Seraglio*] seems to me to epitomize the happy days of youth, whose flowering, once over, can never be recaptured.**‖**
Carl Maria von Weber
1818

Constänze.   *Baffa Sel...*

Pedrillo.   *Das Sarail. Le...*

Der Stumme. Le Mouet.   *Osmin...*

handsome squares; Archduke Maximilian honoured the opening concert with his presence.

But of course it was *The Seraglio* that occupied most of Mozart's time until the end of May. The premiere took place on 16 July. Joseph II's reaction was guarded. 'Too many notes, dear Mozart', he is reputed to have said, though he should have shown himself receptive to the opera's themes of tolerance and generosity enhanced by a score that scintillated with the exuberance of youth and exalted liberty and love. The public was ecstatic. *The Seraglio* was given sixteen performances within a few months: 'My opera was presented yesterday for the third time...to the greatest applause; and again, in spite of the dreadful heat, the theatre was packed. ... I may say that people are quite mad about this opera. It really does one good to be so applauded' (letter of 27 July 1782).

Was it by chance that the heroine with whom Belmonte and Pasha Selim are in love is called Constanze? It would be a mistake to seize on this coincidence too readily. The young couple had just gone through a difficult time. Frau Weber had forced her future son-in-law to sign a contract committing him to pay her daughter 300 florins a year if he broke the engagement. Constanze immediately tore up the document but the memory remained.

E ngravings (centre) of the characters and silhouettes (below) of some of the leading singers in the Vienna premiere of *The Seraglio*. There are five sung roles, a spoken one, and two parts for actors.

5.

Belmonte.

8.

Blonde.

11.

Schiffskapitän.
capitaine du vaisseau.

Therese Teyber   *Valent. Adamberger*

Catarina Cavalieri

Ernst Dauer

Mozart marries Constanze

The couple were married on 4 August 1782 in
St Stephen's Cathedral. Leopold's blessing did not
arrive until the next day. Wolfgang had just finished
his Symphony no. 35, K.385, the *Haffner*, written to
a commission from the Haffner family, but his
prospects were still uncertain; no gesture came from
Joseph II and his court, and he briefly considered
trying his luck in France or England. Constanze
found that she was pregnant. Then the summer was
over and the lessons and concerts resumed. Three
more piano concertos appeared, Nos. 11, 12 and 13,
K.413–5. 'These concertos are a happy medium
between being too easy and too difficult', wrote
Mozart to his father on 28 December 1782. 'They are
very brilliant, pleasing to the ear, and natural,
without being vapid. There are passages here and
there from which only the connoisseurs can derive
satisfaction; but these passages are written in such a
way that non-connoisseurs will find them satisfying

St Stephen's Cathedral,
Vienna. Here Mozart
and Constanze were
married on 4 August
1782. In 1791, shortly
before his death, Mozart
secured from the
municipality the title of
unpaid assistant to
Leopold Hoffmann,
Kapellmeister at St
Stephen's, with the
assurance that he should
succeed to the post
when the incumbent
died.

Constanze Mozart: a portrait dated 1802. A reappraisal of Constanze has taken place in recent years, challenging the traditional very disparaging view that she was extravagant and careless; much documentary evidence seems to reveal that she was competent at handling financial affairs and a tireless champion of her husband's music. Friedrich Schlichtegroll, in an obituary of Mozart, reports that Constanze was 'a good mother to the two surviving children born of their union and an entirely worthy wife who sought to prevent Mozart from falling victim to his own excesses and unwise decisions'.

too, without knowing why.' But he expressed a more intimate side of himself in the String Quartet K.387, the first of the set of six he dedicated to Haydn.

The year 1783 began in a mood of elation natural to a young couple (he was twenty-seven, she was nineteen) expecting their first baby. The lessons and concerts were bringing in a sufficient income, and the only slight disappointment was the closure of the German opera, which meant that the Italians came back in force, led openly by Salieri.

In March Wolfgang met Lorenzo da Ponte, a former priest who had been unfrocked for immoral conduct. The encounter was to change his musical life. He renewed contact with Varesco, the librettist of *Idomeneo*, suggesting they meet in Salzburg. Mozart's last visit to his native city lasted three months: an awkward, uneasy time for Constanze and also for her husband, who was technically still in the employ of Colloredo since no document existed to prove otherwise. During these three months Mozart wrote the Duos for Violin and Viola K.423–4 to help Michael Haydn, who was unwell, and arranged a performance of his incomplete Mass in C minor, K.427, composed in fulfilment of a vow made once when Constanze was ill, before their marriage.

They had not brought Raimund Leopold, their 'fine sturdy baby, round as a ball', born on 17 June while his father was busy finishing the second of the 'Haydn' quartets (K.421). They had no wish to prolong their Salzburg stay; the three months were up at the end of October. They returned via Linz, where Wolfgang composed his Symphony no. 36, K.425, in four days to thank Count Thun for his hospitality. News of a calamity awaited them on their return: the baby was dead.

Vienna continues to treat Mozart well

Despite his grief Mozart remained buoyant. He wrote four more piano concertos, two for his talented new pupil Babette Ployer (No. 14, K.449 and No. 17, K.453) and two whirlwind ones for himself to play (No. 15, K.450 and No. 16, K.451). Time flew by; soon it was the summer of 1784 and another baby was imminent. In Salzburg Nannerl married at last, into the minor aristocracy. She never saw her brother again.

Mozart had met more musicians, including two eminent composers, Giuseppe Sarti and Giovanni Paisiello, and a troupe of English singers including Nancy Storace. On 21 September Karl Thomas was

An 18th-century string quartet session. Mozart wrote 23 quartets between 1770 and 1790.

EINLASS - KARTE ZUM CONCERT von W. A. Mozart.

Ticket for a subscription concert given by Mozart in Vienna in the 1780s.

born. The winter season got under way, with academy concerts which constantly required new compositions, but there was also time for friends, with chamber music sessions in which Dittersdorf and Joseph Haydn played the violins, Mozart the viola and Vanhal the cello. These were favourite moments for Mozart, who was just finishing the set of quartets begun in 1782.

Nancy Storace (1765-1817), the first Susanna in *The Marriage of Figaro.*

1785, an exceptionally productive year

His creativity flowed on, but he took an important decision, the result of long reflection: on 14 December 1784 he became a Freemason at the lodge 'Zur Wohlthätigkeit' ('Beneficence'). February 1785 brought a surprise visit from Leopold, who was moved to tears when Haydn declared that his son was the greatest composer he knew.

Meeting of a Masonic lodge in Vienna, 1790. The figure at the far right has been identified as Mozart. The Masonic hierarchy had three degrees for the spiritual progress of members: Apprentice, Fellow and Master. Each degree had its own visual symbols. Mozart progressed rapidly up the hierarchy, though the date when he became a Master is not known. Freemasonry imposed certain rules and duties on its members. The influence of Masonic thought, especially the ideals of brotherhood and charity, is clear in his later works, which contain a wealth of Masonic symbolism. His first Masonic song, *Zur Gesellenreise* (*The Companions' Journey*, K.468), written in 1785, probably for the ceremony marking his promotion to the Second Degree, is in two flats; pieces referring to Master Masons, such as the cantata *Die Maurerfreude* (*The Masons' Joy*, K.471), are in three flats; Apprenticeship is symbolized by the key of F, which has only one flat. Masonic music also contains characteristic rhythmic and formal features.

His arrival coincided with the finishing of the sublime, tragic Piano Concerto no. 20, K.466, followed immediately by the radiant Piano Concerto no. 21, K.467.

Of course Wolfgang had not forgotten about opera, but he had found no libretto as yet. Da Ponte had proposed *Lo sposo deluso* (*The Deluded Spouse*) but had only jotted down a few ideas. A German opera was out of the question for the moment. Then in 1784 a seditious new comedy by Beaumarchais caused a furore in Paris: it was called *The Marriage of Figaro*. The Emperor promptly banned it from the national theatre in Vienna, but Wolfgang, attracted by the subject-matter, suggested it to Da Ponte, who promised to talk Joseph round. Mozart worked on the opera during the latter part of the year, producing another piano concerto meanwhile (No. 22, K.482). He had to keep the money coming in: their financial situation seemed to be getting worse. In response to a request from the Emperor he also wrote a one-act Singspiel, *Der Schauspieldirektor* (*The Impresario*), performed at Schönbrunn Palace on 7 February 1786 in an evening which also included Salieri's *Prima la musica e poi le parole* (*First the Music, then the Words*).

Mozart, now thirty, begins to feel his artistic isolation

Two more piano concertos, No. 23, K.488, and the lesser-known but magnificent No. 24, K.491,

The humanity and wit of *The Marriage of Figaro* have made it one of the most perenially popular of all operas. Mozart wrote most of it in a house in the Domgasse, Vienna (left). Right: set for Act IV by Hans Frahm. Below: 19th-century costumes for Cherubino and Susanna.

appeared in March, and then on 1 May 1786, at the Burgtheater, despite the cabals, came the premiere of *The Marriage of Figaro*. It was only a qualified success. Some of the audience were wildly enthusiastic but others were not, for the audacity of the dramatic situations and the originality of the music did not altogether appeal to Vienna's trivial-minded public. His most personal work, the remarkable string quartets dedicated to Haydn, aroused no interest. He felt alone and misunderstood. He was sad too, for their third child, Johann Thomas, born on 16 October, survived only a month. He debated going to England. But hope came from Prague.

• Of all the performers in this opera at that time, but one survives – myself. ... All the original performers had the advantage of the instruction of the composer, who transfused into their minds his inspired meaning. I never shall forget his little animated countenance, when lighted up with the glowing rays of genius; – it is as impossible to describe it, as it would be to paint sun-beams. ... I remember at the first rehearsal of the full band, Mozart was on the stage with his crimson pelisse and gold-laced cocked hat, giving the time of the music to the orchestra.•

Michael Kelly
Reminiscences, 1826

In 1787 Mozart was thirty-one. He had four more years to live – four years during which the financial difficulties that had dogged him for so long continued unabated. These were perhaps the darkest years of his life, yet during them he composed his greatest and most radiant masterpieces.

CHAPTER 6

LIGHT AND DARKNESS

Opposite: this unfinished, enigmatic portrait was painted in 1789–90 by Joseph Lange, husband of Aloysia Weber.

'I must frankly admit that...although Prague is indeed a very beautiful and pleasant place, I long most ardently to be back in Vienna.'

The year 1787 started well. On 11 January Mozart arrived in Prague with Constanze at the invitation of Count Thun, to conduct *The Marriage of Figaro*. It was received with wild enthusiasm and the composer was the toast of the town. He gave a concert of his Symphony no. 38, K.504 (the *Prague*, composed at the same time as the Piano Concerto no. 25) and performed some improvisations, to a hall full to overflowing. When Wolfgang returned to Vienna he had not only the ovations of Prague resounding in his ears, but a commission for a new opera from Pasquale Bondini, the director of the theatre, in his pocket.

The happiness of the Prague stay is followed by hard times

His English friends, including Nancy Storace (creator of the part of Susanna), had left Vienna. The loss of a close friend, Count Hatzfeld, reminded Mozart of the omnipresence of death; he accepted it stoically, but gave expression to his anguish in the sublime String Quintets K.515 and K.516. One April day there was a knock at the door of the humble lodgings to which he had moved: it was a youth of seventeen, organist of the Archbishop of Cologne. His name was Ludwig van Beethoven. This unexpected encounter between two musical giants seems to have left no mark on either.

Fate began to hound him cruelly. Leopold had been ill for some time, but his sudden death on 28 May was a profound shock to Wolfgang. A door had slammed on his past. He had seen his

It was at the Villa Bertramka in Prague, home of Mozart's friends the Duscheks, that he finished *Don Giovanni*. Josepha Duschek was a singer, pianist and composer who continued to perform until well into the 19th century. It is said that she once locked Mozart into a room and refused to release him until he had written her a concert aria. This was *Bella mia fiamma, addio!* ('My beautiful love, farewell!'). Right: Mozart playing on the Duscheks' piano.

sister and Salzburg for the last time. Yet he had to go on working, and in August he produced one of his best-loved compositions, the Serenade K.525, *Eine kleine Nachtmusik* (*A Little Night-Music*), for string quartet plus double-bass.

The new opera made progress during the summer. Da Ponte proposed a libretto for *Don Giovanni* which bore a strong resemblance to *Il convitato di pietra* (*The Stone Guest*) by Giovanni Bertati, set to music by Giuseppe Gazzaniga in 1787 – one

The young Beethoven visits Mozart. Mozart's 19th-century biographer Otto Jahn describes the scene: 'At Mozart's request Beethoven played. Mozart, guessing that it was a party piece learnt by heart, was polite but unimpressed. Beethoven understood, and asked Mozart for a theme on which he could improvise freely. ... He played so brilliantly that Mozart, slipping into the next room where some friends were waiting, exclaimed: "Look out for that man; one day he'll have the world talking about him."'

of many existing treatments of the Don Juan story. In Prague Mozart closely followed the preparations, which did not run smoothly. In fact the score was still not quite completed: legend has it that the overture was not written until two days before the first night on 29 October. But the opera was received with tremendous acclaim. When Mozart returned to Vienna in mid-November the Emperor nominated him 'composer of the Imperial chamber' to replace Gluck, who had recently died – though the remuneration he offered Mozart was noticeably lower.

Mozart and Da Ponte's *Don Giovanni* was first performed in Prague on 29 October 1787 by the Italian opera company. Left and opposite, below: Zerlina and Leporello in an early Paris production. Julius Nisle's lithographs (below and opposite, above) show the Don wooing Zerlina, and the confusion at the end of Act I.

Mozart's star seems to wane as the Viennese public, fickle as ever, lose interest

On 27 December 1787, to his delight, Constanze gave birth to a daughter, Theresia. But their financial problems were going from bad to worse. His attempt to open subscriptions to pay for a concert or the engraving of a new work received no response. It is clear that he had no idea of handling money – he tried to keep accounts for a short while, as well as a catalogue of his works, but it did not last – and Constanze was content to live from hand to mouth, spending money when there was any, and concentrating on keeping up appearances. She was almost continually pregnant; they went from illness to illness, barely keeping their heads above water.

Don Juan, oder: der bestrafte Bösewicht.

In 1788 the deadly cycle of debts began. Mozart's begging letters to his friend Michael Puchberg, a rich merchant and fellow-Mason, are heart-rending.

Vienna continued to shun him: on 7 May *Don Giovanni* was a flop, to Haydn's indignation. It was true that those who applauded Vicente Martín y Soler and Dittersdorf were not likely to respond favourably to a piece where defiant desire leads to death. Joseph II summed up the situation at one of the last performances: 'The opera is divine, I would say it is even more beautiful than *Figaro*; but it is not a meat suitable for the teeth of my Viennese.' To which Mozart is said to have replied: 'Give them time to chew on it!'

Summer 1788 is a time of extraordinary creativity – Mozart's challenge to fate

Up till June Mozart's best composition of 1788 was the brilliant Piano Concerto no. 26, K.537, nicknamed the *Coronation* because it was performed in 1790 at the coronation of Leopold II in Frankfurt. The sadnesses of recent years were reflected in the deeply poignant Adagio for Piano in B minor, K.540, written on 19 March. Now in the summer Mozart produced a string of masterpieces, the first of which was the Piano Trio no. 5 in E major, K.542, commissioned by Puchberg, followed by two others. More remarkable even than the Divertimento for String Trio K.563, dedicated to his friend and creditor, was the sequence of the three last symphonies. No. 39 in E flat, K.543, was finished on 26 June 1788 – three days before the death of his daughter. He completed the tragic No. 40 in G minor, K.550, on 25 July and No. 41 in C, K.551 – the superb *Jupiter* – on 10 August. One is struck by the strength of Mozart's determination, mirrored in this progression, to triumph over

Joseph II died on 20 February 1790. He was succeeded by his brother Leopold II (left), formerly Grand Duke of Tuscany, who was to reign only two years. Joseph II's wish had been to be remembered as a monarch who was sensitive to the main concerns of his time and his subjects, even if it meant offending the nobility by attacking their privileges; Leopold was much more cautious and less idealistic. It must be remembered that the French Revolution threw everything into confusion.

personal disaster, and by his unquenchable confidence, no doubt fortified by the philosophical precepts of Freemasonry. Mozart did not give in. He fought on his own terms for what mattered to him above all else: his music.

The next six months are devoted to earning his bread

The German Dances written next for the court were charming but not especially distinguished. More interesting was a task given him by Baron van Swieten, who, still infatuated with Bach and Handel, declared the wish to let the Viennese hear their great oratorios in an up-to-date orchestration. Mozart accordingly took the score of Handel's *Acis and Galatea* and replaced the organ by wind instruments. He also made changes to *Messiah*, turning some of the arias into recitatives. Van Swieten was pleased, but the work was unworthy of Mozart's genius and did not even bring in much money.

In 1789 Constanze was pregnant for the fifth time and the household's finances were in as parlous a state as ever. A chance seemed to present itself in April

After Mozart's death, Constanze dedicated the score of one of his piano concertos to the music-loving Prince Ludwig Ferdinand of Prussia (1772–1806), a friend of Beethoven.

when a former pupil, Prince Karl Lichnowsky, left for Berlin and suggested that Mozart accompany him. On the way they passed through Prague, where Mozart called on the Duscheks; through Dresden, where he performed at court and at the residence of the Russian ambassador (who found him 'very learned, very difficult, and consequently very esteemed by instrumentalists'); and through Leipzig, where he played J. S. Bach's organ in St Thomas'.

Only two of the six children born to Wolfgang and Constanze survived infancy. Karl Thomas (right) went into administration and Franz Xaver Wolfgang became a composer, signing his works 'Wolfgang Amadeus Mozart'. Both remained bachelors and died childless. This portrait dates from 1798.

On 25 April his attention turned to the court of Potsdam. Frederick William II of Prussia was, like his late uncle Frederick the Great, a music-lover. He later maintained that Mozart had refused his offer of the post of Kapellmeister. Whatever the truth of this assertion, he certainly welcomed the composer cordially and commissioned string quartets and piano sonatas for his daughter Frederike. But Mozart only stayed seven days. Following Lichnowsky, he left on 2 May, stopping again in Leipzig to give a recital at the Gewandhaus on the 12th. He quarrelled with the prince, however, and – contrary to plans and economic prudence – returned to Berlin, where he appeared before the queen.

St Thomas' Church, Leipzig, where J. S. Bach had been cantor.

Wolfgang returns home after a two-month absence, poorer than ever

Constanze was suffering from an infected foot and had to go to take the waters at Baden: heavy expense was in prospect, and again he was forced to ask for loans: 'I beg and implore you, in God's name, for whatever temporary help you can give me' (letter to Puchberg, 17 July 1789).

Frederick William II of Prussia, cellist and lover of chamber music.

The Marriage of Figaro was revived in August, bringing with it a note of relief, for it led to a commission from the Emperor. Joseph II himself chose the subject for a new opera, *Così fan tutte, ossia La scuola degli amanti* ('Women are all the Same, or The School for Lovers'), traditionally inspired by an anecdote which was going the rounds of the salons. Da Ponte wrote the libretto. They worked fast: the premiere was planned for January 1790. Puchberg and Haydn followed its progress with an affectionate eye and some concern, as the last months of the year were clouded by tragedy: another baby, Anna Maria, born on 16 November, lived only an hour. Yet Mozart found time to respond to a request from a fellow-Mason, the clarinettist Anton Stadler, with the Clarinet Quintet K.581. The voice of Mozart's

The opera *Così fan tutte* is Mozart's most complex exploration of truth, falsehood, fidelity and betrayal. Here one of the heroes, disguised as an Albanian, woos his friend's fiancée.

Introduzzione

The silhouette typifies the fun-loving Dorabella as she sings of the pranks of Cupid in her Act II aria, 'E amore un ladroncello' ('Love is a little thief').

favourite instrument soars with sublime lyricism in this work, which heralded the masterpieces of the two final years.

Despite the cabals engineered by Salieri, *Così fan tutte* is produced

The new opera was performed on 26 January 1790. Its favourable reception was mingled with some incomprehension: its subject was considered amusing, its subtle cruelty not fully appreciated. Another calamity now occurred; the death of the Emperor. He had been a reliable protector if not a generous one; his successor Leopold II, though he kept Mozart on, paid little attention to him – just at a time when Mozart so sorely needed aid. For, burdened by his financial worries, his health had begun to suffer. He wrote little during 1790, indeed nothing between January and May, when he finished the last two quartets in the set dedicated to the King of Prussia.

He had applied for the post of assistant Kapellmeister, but was turned down. The new

Playbill for the premiere of *Così*. The conflict between desire and commitment at the heart of the opera was not fully understood, and in the 19th century the music was given a different set of words. Yet the fundamental ambiguity of *Così* constitutes its greatest appeal to a modern audience.

sovereign's lack of interest in him was proved conclusively when, unlike his colleagues, Mozart was not invited either to the celebrations in honour of Ferdinand and Maria Carolina of Naples, or to Leopold's coronation at Frankfurt on 9 October. He went all the same at his own expense, pawning silver and furniture.

The last months: misery and divine inspiration

Hardly had he returned to Vienna than a new chance came up: he was asked to write two operas for London. But he would have had to spend six months in the English capital, and how was he to do this with no money? He had to refuse, and with tears in his eyes watched Joseph Haydn setting off, engaged by the impresario Johann Peter Salomon. Yet he pulled himself together and began to compose again and look for pupils. He also began to accept the idea of another birth. He wrote the String Quintet K.593 and then the Piano Concerto no. 27, K.595, the last in this brilliant series. Far from betraying his sufferings, these works seem to contain a new verve and popular appeal. In March came some good news: Emanuel Schikaneder, who had taken over as director of the Theater auf der Wieden in 1789, gave him the libretto of *The Magic Flute*, which Mozart accepted with alacrity. Constanze had gone back to Baden. He joined her for a few days in June, concerned about her health; but apart from that, he stayed in Vienna working.

Playbill announcing the premiere of *The Magic Flute*. Fairytale, philosophical fable, Masonic opera – it was all these and more.

Papageno the bird-catcher, in an engraving of 1791 (left), and two scenes from *The Magic Flute*, c. 1793 (opposite): Papageno charms the animals, and Sarastro appears.

The model for the wise high priest Sarastro was probably Count Ignaz von Born, Mason and eminent mineralogist, who came to Vienna at the request of Maria Theresa. Mozart wrote the cantata *The Masons' Joy*, performed in 1785, in his honour.

Genesis of a masterpiece

Mozart had not expected to have another opportunity to write a German opera, but Emanuel Schikaneder suggested the idea of *The Magic Flute* to him. Sources for the plot include *Sethos*, a novel by Jean Terrasson, and Paul Wranitzky's opera *Oberon, King of the Elves*. Schikaneder wrote most of the libretto and also sang Papageno in the premiere. This set design for the palace of the Queen of the Night is by the great German architect Karl Friedrich Schinkel, for a Berlin production of 1816. Below: a 19th-century Sarastro.

The stuff of heroes

The plot of *The Magic Flute* centres on three couples. The young hero Tamino is willing to endure unflinchingly the tests and trials of initiation at the side of his beloved Pamina. Papageno, the bird-catcher, may be seen as Tamino's counterpart: for all his enduring naïvety and childlike common sense, he is ready to die if he cannot find his Papagena. The wise Sarastro, symbol of light and goodness, confronts and finally overcomes the power of darkness represented by the Queen of the Night. Left: set for Sarastro's garden, by Schinkel. Below: Monostatos, Sarastro's Moorish servant.

The imprint of Freemasonry

In its story *The Magic Flute* seems an oriental fairytale, with its monsters, genies and metamorphoses, but it reflects the Masonic interests of both composer and librettist: these are evident in the initiation ritual which the chief protagonists undergo, the allusions to ancient Egypt, and the number symbolism. The work's message of love, brotherhood and sublime wisdom transcends such specific details. Left: the Queen of the Night, as conceived by Simon Quaglio for Munich, 1818. Below: the same character in another 19th-century production.

Seriously ill, Mozart throws his last energies into two operas

Schikaneder kept an eye on him and lent him a summer-house near the theatre, where Mozart could compose and relax with a circle of friends. On 26 July his sixth child, Franz Xaver Wolfgang, was born.

At about the same time Mozart received an unsigned letter containing a commission for a requiem mass. It has become the subject of endless speculation, but is in fact easily explained: a certain Count Franz von Walsegg, who fancied himself as a composer, wanted a requiem for his late wife, to be passed off as his own work. The mysterious stranger who delivered the order was his servant. Mozart was exhausted; he still had *The Magic Flute* to complete, and he had received a new commission from the National Theatre in Prague for an opera to celebrate the coronation of Leopold II as King of Bohemia on 6 September. Yet he agreed to write the *Requiem*.

The composition of *La clemenza di Tito* ('The Clemency of Titus'), his last Italian opera, to a libretto by Metastasio revised by Caterino Mazzolà, took eighteen days from start to finish. He worked at it constantly, even during the journey. He was delighted to be back in Prague, which he liked so much and where he was truly appreciated. He returned to Vienna in mid-September, tired out.

But he had to finish *The Magic Flute* in time for its premiere on 30 September, and he did. It was a triumph. The theatre was packed and the audience, which consisted of townspeople rather than the ladies and gentlemen of the salons, gave it a huge ovation. This was his last opera.

Mozart writes the *Requiem*

Mozart was worn out. He used his remaining strength to compose two more works, the Clarinet Concerto K.622, written for Stadler, and the *Requiem*. In this last work, as in *La clemenza di Tito*, he was helped by his pupil Franz Xaver Süssmayr. They worked

● His last movement was an attempt to express with his mouth a drum passage in the *Requiem*. I can hear it still.●

Sophie Haibel,
Mozart's sister-in-law
1825

desperately. By the end of November his illness had him in its grip: his hands and feet were swollen and partly paralysed. He made one last effort to finish the work. But the manuscript breaks off after the eighth bar of the *Lacrymosa*.

On 4 December his condition deteriorated further, and he knew he was about to die. Priests were summoned, but hesitated to come to the death-bed of a Freemason. Mozart remained calm. Late that evening he fell into a coma. The end came just before one o'clock in the morning. He received the plainest of funerals. A few devoted friends followed the simple cortège, but not Constanze, who was too exhausted. The body was placed in a communal grave without even a cross.

●I have come to the end before having enjoyed my talent. Life was so lovely, my career opened under such happy auspices, but one cannot change one's destiny. No one can know the measure of his days; one must resign oneself, for it will all go as Providence decrees. I end my days; here is my requiem which I must not leave unfinished.●

Mozart
September 1791

DOCUMENTS

A mere thirty-five years – an extraordinary life,
documented not only by musical works:
fascinating correspondence, vivid portraits
sketched by contemporaries, and varied
assessments by composers, critics and performers
all build up a rounded picture.

Correspondence

Wolfgang's letters from 1769 on tell frankly of his joys and troubles, frustrations and struggles. Like his compositions, they are full of sensitivity and tenderness.

Having just completed his opera 'Lucio Silla' Wolfgang relaxes by adding a postscript to a letter to his sister from their father. He writes in the comic vein peculiar to him.

[Milan, 18 December 1772]
To Nannerl

I hope you are well, my dear sister. When you receive this letter, my dear sister, my opera will be being performed that same evening. Think of me, my dear sister, and do your best to imagine, my dear sister, that you are watching and hearing it too, my dear sister. Admittedly that is difficult as it is already eleven o'clock; what's more, I believe beyond any doubt that during the day it is brighter than at Easter. My dear sister, tomorrow we dine at Herr von Mayer's, and why is this, do you think? Guess! Because he has invited us. Tomorrow's rehearsal is at the theatre, but the impresario, Signor Castiglioni, has urged me not to say anything about it, because otherwise everybody will come rushing along, and we don't want that. So, my child, I beg you not to tell anyone anything about it. Otherwise too many people would come rushing along. That reminds me, do you know what happened here today? I'll tell you. We left Count Firmian's to go home and when we reached our street, we opened the front door and what do you suppose happened then? We went in. Goodbye, my little lung. I embrace you, my liver, and remain, my stomach, ever your unworthy brother *frater*

Wolfgang

Please, my dear sister, something is biting me – please scratch me.

Leopold and Wolfgang Mozart.

The Hannibal Platz (now Makart Platz), Salzburg, lies across the river from the cathedral and castle. The Mozarts moved into the house on the right in 1773, and Leopold lived there until his death in 1787. In the background are the domed church of the Holy Trinity and a hill crowned by the Capuchin monastery.

This petition from Wolfgang to Count Hieronymus Colloredo, Prince-Archbishop of Salzburg, was actually written by Leopold and signed by his son. A pencil note in the Archbishop's hand reads: 'To the Court Chamberlain with my decision that father and son have my firm permission to seek their fortune elsewhere.'

1 August 1777
Your Grace, most worthy Prince of the Holy Roman Empire!

I will not presume to trouble Your Grace with a detailed description of our unhappy circumstances, of which my father respectfully gave an exact account in his humble petition which was handed to you on 14 March 1777. As, however, your hoped-for consent was not forthcoming, my father intended last June most respectfully to beg Your Grace once more to allow us to travel for a few months in order to recover our fortunes somewhat; and he would have done so, if Your Grace had not given orders that in view of the pending visit of His Majesty the Emperor your orchestra should hold itself in readiness for all contingencies. Later my father again respectfully requested leave of absence, but Your Grace refused it, your gracious decision being that I, who am in any case only half in your service, could travel alone. Our situation is pressing; my father therefore decided to let me go on my own. But even so Your Grace has been pleased to raise certain objections. Most gracious Prince and Lord! Parents endeavour to endow their children with the ability to earn their own bread, and they should do this in their own interest and that of the State. The greater the talents which children have received from God, the more they ought to use them to improve their own circumstances and those of their parents, to stand by their parents and to work towards their own advancement and a secure future. The Gospel instructs us on this proper use of talents. My conscience tells me that I owe it to God to be grateful to my father, who has spent his time tirelessly on my education, so that I may lighten his burden and provide for myself and later on for my sister. For I should be sorry to think that she had spent so many hours at the harpsichord and was still unable to make the best use of her training.

Your Grace will therefore be so good as to allow me to ask you most humbly for leave of absence, which I should like to take at the beginning of autumn, so that I am not exposed to the inclement weather of the coming winter months. Your Grace will not receive this petition ungraciously, for when I asked you for permission to travel to Vienna three years ago, you graciously declared that I had nothing to hope for in Salzburg and would do better to seek my fortune elsewhere. I thank your Grace most respectfully for all the favours I have received from you, and, with the earnest hope of being able to serve you in my mature years with greater success,

I remain your most humble
and obedient servant
Wolfgang Amadé Mozart

Mozart was slow in replying to his father's letters.

Paris, 31 July 1778

Monsieur mon très cher père!

… M. Grimm said to me the other day: 'What am I to tell your father? What course do you intend to pursue? Are you staying here or going to Mannheim?' I really could not help laughing. 'What am I supposed to do in Mannheim now?' I said, 'I wish I had never come to Paris – but so it is. I am here and I must use every effort to make a success of it.' 'Well,' he said, 'I hardly think that you will achieve much in Paris.' 'Why not?' I asked. 'I see a crowd of second-rate bunglers getting on fine; why shouldn't I, with my talents?'… 'Well,' he said, 'I am afraid that you are not being sufficiently active here – you do not get about enough.'…

What annoys me most of all is that these stupid French people seem to think I am still seven years old, because that was my age when they first saw me. They treat me as a beginner – except of course the real musicians, who think differently. But it is the majority that counts.

I shall do my utmost to get along here by teaching and to earn as much money as possible, which I am now doing in the fond hope that my circumstances may soon change; for I cannot deny, and must confess, that I should be delighted to be released from this place. Giving lessons here is no joke. It is exhausting; unless you take a large number of pupils, you cannot make much money. You must not think that this is laziness on my part – not at all. It just goes completely against my genius and the way I live. You know

A silk writing-case which belonged to Mozart.

that I have my being, so to speak, entirely in music, I am immersed in it all day long and love to try out ideas, work on them and mull them over. Well, I am prevented from doing this by my way of life here. True, I shall have a few hours free, but I shall need those few hours more for rest than for work. I told you in my last letter about the opera. I cannot help it – I must write a full-scale opera or none at all. If I write a small one, I shall get very little for it (for everything is taxed here). And should it have the misfortune not to please these stupid French, all would be over – I would never get the chance to compose another – I would have gained nothing by it – and my reputation would have suffered. If, on the other hand, I write a full-length opera, the remuneration will be better – I shall be doing the work I like best and am best at – and I shall have better hopes of success, for with a large-scale work you have a better chance of making your name. I assure you that if I am commissioned to write an opera, I shall have no qualms at all. True, this language [i.e., French] is an invention of the devil – and I fully realize the difficulties which all composers have encountered. But in spite of this I feel I am just as capable of overcoming them as anyone else. On the contrary, whenever I fancy, as I often do, that I have got the commission, my whole body seems to be on fire and I tremble from head to foot with eagerness to teach the French more thoroughly to know, appreciate and fear the Germans. For why is a full-length opera never entrusted to a Frenchman? Why must it always be a foreigner? For me the most detestable aspect would be the singers. Well, I am ready – I wish to avoid quarrels – but if I am challenged, I shall know how to defend myself. But I should prefer to avoid a duel, for I do not care to wrestle with dwarfs.

Wolfgang Amadé Mozart

As time went on, a rupture with the Archbishop of Salzburg became inevitable. Mozart longed for it and, desperate for liberty, finally provoked it. He reports to his father:

Vienna, 9 May 1781

Mon très cher père!

I am still seething with rage! And I am sure that you, my dearest and most beloved father, are equally angry with me. My patience has been tried for so long that at last it has given out. I am no longer so unfortunate as to be in Salzburg service. Today is a happy day for me. I'll tell you what happened.

Twice already that – I don't know what to call him – has said to my face the greatest *sottises* and *impertinences*, which I did not repeat to you, out of consideration for your feelings, and for which I only refrained from taking my revenge at the time because you, my dear father, were ever before my eyes. He called me a lout and a dissolute wretch and told me to be off. And I – endured it all, although I felt that not only my honour but yours too was being attacked. But, in accordance with your wish, I remained silent. Now read this.

A week ago a footman came up unexpectedly and told me to clear out that very instant. All the others had been informed of the day of their departure, all but me. So I hastily threw everything into my trunk, and old

The square known as the Graben, at the heart of Vienna. The city was ideal for a composer: the Viennese loved celebrations, and music was an important part of daily life.

Madame Weber has been good enough to take me into her house. I have a lovely room, and I am living with people who are obliging and who supply me with all the things which one often requires in a hurry and which one does not have when living alone. …

When I presented myself today, the valets informed me that the Archbishop wanted to give me a parcel to take charge of. I asked whether it was urgent. They told me, 'Yes, it is of the greatest importance.' ... When I went in to the Archbishop...his first words were: *Archbishop*: 'Well, boy, when are you leaving?' *I*: 'I intended to go tonight, but all the seats were already taken.' That started him off – I was the most despicable wretch he knew – no one served him as badly as I did – he advised me to leave today or else he would write home and have my salary stopped. I couldn't get a word in edgeways, for he raged on like a fire. I listened to it all without losing control. He lied to my face that my salary was five hundred gulden, called me a scoundrel, an oaf, a good-for-nothing. Oh, I really do not wish to tell you all he said. At last my blood began to boil and I said, 'So Your Grace is not satisfied with me?' 'What, are you threatening me – you scoundrel? There is the door! I want nothing more to do with you, you wretched youth.' At last I said: 'Nor I with you!' 'Well, get out then!' On my way out, I said, 'This is final. You shall have it tomorrow in writing.'

Tell me now, my dear father, did I not speak out too late rather than too soon? The point is, my honour means more to me than anything else and I know that you feel the same. Do not worry about me at all. I am so sure of my success here [in Vienna] that I would have left even without the slightest reason; and since I now have a very good reason to do so – in fact three reasons – I have nothing to gain by delaying any longer. On the contrary – I had played the coward twice and I just could not do so a third time.

As long as the Archbishop remains here, I shall not give a concert. You seem convinced that I am putting myself in a bad light with the Emperor and the nobility, but that is quite wrong; the Archbishop is hated here, and by the Emperor most of all. ... By the next post I shall send you a little money to show you that I am not starving. Now please be cheerful, for my happiness is just beginning, and I trust that my happiness will be yours also. Write to me in cypher that you are pleased – and indeed you really can be pleased – but in public find fault with me as much as you like, so that no blame falls on you. ...

I want nothing more to do with Salzburg. I hate the Archbishop to distraction.

Adieu. I kiss your hands a thousand times and embrace my dear sister with all my heart and am ever your obedient son.

The composition of 'The Seraglio' took nearly a year; it was held up because Mozart insisted that Gottlieb Stephanie should partially re-write the libretto. In this letter to his father he explains his conception of the relationship of words to music.

Vienna
13 October 1781

Mon très cher père!

... It is my view that in an opera the poetry must be without question the obedient daughter of the music. Why are Italian comic operas so popular everywhere – in spite of their miserable libretti – even in Paris, where I myself witnessed their success? Because the music is all-important and when one listens to it one forgets everything else. An opera is all the more sure of success when the plot is well worked out and the words are written solely for the music and not added here and there for the sake of some silly rhyme which, God knows, contributes nothing to the value of any theatrical performance, whatever it is, but rather detracts from it – I mean, words or even entire verses which ruin the composer's whole concept. Verse is indeed the most indispensable element for music – but rhymes for their own sake are the most detrimental. Those pretentious people who set to work in this pedantic fashion will always come to grief, and so will their music. The best thing of all is when a good composer, who understands the stage and is talented enough to have ideas of his own, comes across a skilful poet, that true phoenix; then one need have no worries even concerning the applause of the ignorant. Librettists seem to me almost like trumpeters with their tricks of the trade! If we composers were always to stick just as faithfully to our rules (which were good enough at a time when no one knew better), we would be producing music just as mediocre as their mediocre libretti.

Well, I think I have chattered enough nonsense to you; so I must now enquire about what is dearest of all to me: your health, my dearest father! ...

I trust that my sister is improving daily. I kiss her with all my heart and, my dearest, most beloved father, I kiss your hands a thousand times and am ever your most obedient son

W. A. Mozart

Mozart writes to his father to inform him of his decision to marry Constanze Weber.

Vienna, 15 December 1781

Dearest father,

You demand an explanation of the words at the end of my last letter. How gladly I would have opened my heart to you long ago, but I was discouraged from doing so by the reproach which I knew you might have made me for *thinking about such a thing at an inappropriate time* – although to think can never be inappropriate. My efforts in the meantime are directed to acquiring a small but *steady* income here, for then one can live quite well with the help of the irregular extra sums; and then I intend – to marry! Are you appalled at the idea? But, dear, kind father, please read on. I have had to reveal to you what is on my mind; now allow me to reveal my reasons too. The voice of nature speaks just as loudly in me as in anyone else, perhaps louder than in many a big strong lout. It is impossible for me to live as most young men do today; in the first place, I am too deeply religious, secondly I am too compassionate and too honourable to wish to lead some innocent girl astray, and thirdly I have too much horror and revulsion, fear and apprehension of disease, and solicitude for my health, to romp about with whores, and I can swear to never having done such a thing. ... I know that this reason, strong though it is, is not sufficient in itself. But my temperament, which is more inclined towards a peaceful domestic existence than to riotous living – I who from my childhood have never been accustomed to look after my own things – clothes, linen and so on – can think of nothing I need more than a wife. I assure you that I often spend more money than necessary because I do not pay heed to those things – I am quite convinced that with a wife, and the same income that I have as a single man, I would manage better. How much needless expenditure would then be avoided? – true, one then has other expenses, but one knows what they are and can allow for them – in short, one can lead a well-regulated life. A bachelor, to my mind, lives only half a life. That is my mind and I cannot change it. ...

So who, then, is the object of my love? Once again, please do not be appalled – surely not one of the Webers? Yes, one of the Webers – not Josepha, not Sophie, but Costanza, the middle one. ... My dear, good Constanze is the martyr of the family, and is, perhaps for that very reason, the kindest, most capable, in short the best of them all. ...

She is not ugly but not at all beautiful. Her beauty consists entirely in two little dark eyes and a lovely figure. She is not witty, but she has enough common sense to be able to fulfil her duties as a wife and mother. She is not inclined to be extravagant; it would be quite wrong to say she was. On the contrary, she is used to being poorly clad, for whatever their mother had to spare was always given to the others, never to her. She would like to be nicely, neatly dressed, but does not aspire to elegance. Most of what a young lady requires she can do for herself, and she always dresses her own hair. She understands household economy and has the kindest heart in the world – I love her and she genuinely loves me. Tell me, could I wish for a better wife? ...

I kiss your hands a thousand times and am ever your obedient son

W. A. Mozart

The Theresienbaden, a bathing establishment in the spa town of Baden near Vienna, seen in Mozart's time.

Mozart's condition, both physical and material, went from bad to worse. He wrote numerous letters containing urgent requests for money to his fellow-Mason Michael Puchberg, who seems to have been the only person he could turn to.

Vienna, 17 May 1790

Dearest friend and brother Mason,

… I am at the moment so devoid of funds that I must beg you, dearest friend, in God's name, to support me with however much you can spare. If, as I hope, I get the other money in a week or two, I will immediately repay what you lend me now – as to what I have owed you for so long already, I must ask you to continue to be patient. If you only knew what grief and worry all this causes me – it has prevented me all this time from finishing my quartets. … Next Saturday I intend to perform my quartets at my home, and you and your wife are most cordially invited. Dearest, best friend and brother, please do not withdraw your friendship on account of my importunity, but stand by me. I rely wholly on you and remain ever yours in deepest gratitude,

Mozart

I have two pupils at present and should like to increase the number to eight – please spread the word that I am willing to give lessons.

In 1791 Constanze was ill and had to go for a cure at Baden. Mozart, full of solicitude, wrote to her every day.

Vienna
Wednesday 6 July 1791

Dearest, most beloved little wife,

I received with indescribable pleasure the news that you had received the money safely. I cannot remember writing to you that you should settle *all* the bills! How could I, a rational creature, have written that? But so it is – I must have done it without thinking, which is quite possible as I have so many important things on my mind just now. My intention was *only* that you should pay for your *baths* – the rest was for your own use, and as for the remaining expenses, which I have already reckoned up, I will deal with them when I arrive. ... Our life is not exactly very enjoyable. But let's be patient – I'm sure things will improve, and then I shall rest in your arms!

At the moment you can give me no greater pleasure than by being cheerful and content – for if I know for sure that *you have all you need*, then all my efforts are a pleasure to be welcomed; the direst, most difficult situation I might find myself in would present no problem if I know that you are *in good health and spirits*. Farewell... think of me and talk of me often – love me forever as I love you, and be ever my Stanzi Marini, as I shall ever be your
Stu! – Knaller paller –
schnip – schnap – schnur –
Schnepeperl.
snai! –

Give X. a box on the ears and tell him you were trying to swat a fly that I had spied on his face! Farewell. Watch now – catch — bi – bi – bi – three kisses, sweet as sugar, are flying towards you!

Mozart writes again to Constanze at Baden. In this letter, as in the previous one, 'X.' represents a name crossed out in the letter by a later hand.

Vienna
7 July 1791

Dearest, most beloved little wife!

You will forgive me, I know, for only sending you one letter a day. The reason is that I must keep track of X. and not let him escape. I am at his house every day at seven o'clock in the morning.

I hope you got the letter I wrote you yesterday. ... My one wish now is to get my affairs settled so that I can be with you again. You cannot imagine how dreadfully I have been missing you all this time. I can't describe what I have been feeling – a kind of emptiness which is really painful – a kind of longing, which is never satisfied and never ceases, which persists and indeed increases day by day. When I think what fun we had together at Baden, like a pair of children, and what sad, weary hours I am spending here! Even my work gives me no pleasure, because I am accustomed to break off from working now and then and exchange a few words with you – a pleasure which, sadly, is not possible now. If I go to the piano and sing something out of my opera [*The Magic Flute*], I have to stop at once, as I get overcome by emotion. Basta! The very hour after I finish this business I shall be up and away from here.

I have no news to tell you. ...

Adieu, dearest little wife. Ever your
Mozart

Mozart through the eyes of his contemporaries

Many accounts of Mozart survive, in pen portraits by relatives, friends, and comparative strangers, including one whose interest was primarily scientific. All have in common the sense of wonder at coming into contact with the inexplicable phenomenon of genius.

As a child, Mozart's sister Maria Anna ('Nannerl') played the keyboard as brilliantly as her brother, but after she had turned sixteen Leopold left her behind when he took Wolfgang abroad. There was no thought of a career for her as a professional musician, simply because of her sex. She tried her hand at composing and was enthusiastically encouraged by Wolfgang, but her efforts were ignored by Leopold. Particularly after Wolfgang's marriage the two seem rarely to have met or corresponded, perhaps partly because she shared her father's disapproval of Constanze. In 1792, after Wolfgang's death, she provided information about him for his publishers at their request: her accounts preserve a cool, studied objectivity.

Wolfgang was small, thin, pale, and totally unremarkable in both face and figure. Except in music he was and remained more or less a child, and this is a dominant feature of the negative side of his character. He would always have needed a father, mother or other mentor; he could not manage money; and he married, against his father's wishes, a girl who was quite unsuitable for him – hence the great disorder in the household at the time of his death and afterwards.

From childhood on he used to play and compose at night-time and in the early morning. If he sat down at the keyboard at 9 o'clock it was impossible to get him away from it before midnight. I believe he would have played all night. Between six and nine in the morning he generally composed

L eopold, Wolfgang and Nannerl performing in Paris in 1763.

in bed, then he got up and composed nothing throughout the day unless a composition was required in a great hurry. ... I do not remember him ever practising after the age of seven, for his practice consisted in playing to other people: he liked pieces to be put before him which he would then sight-read. That was how he practised.

Maria Anna Mozart
letter to Friedrich Schlichtegroll
in *Mozart. Briefe und Aufzeichnungen*,
ed. W. A. Bauer and O. E. Deutsch,
IV, 1962

Andreas Schachtner, court trumpeter at Salzburg and a close friend of the family, recalled memories of Wolfgang as a little boy of seven, in a letter written on 24 April 1794 to Maria Anna Mozart.

You ask what your late brother's favourite pastimes were when he was a child, when he was not making music. No reply is possible to this question; for as soon as he had become devoted to music, all his senses were as if dead to all else, and even the usual childish games and amusements had to be accompanied by music if they were to hold his attention; if he and I ever took toys or games from one room to another, whichever of us was empty-handed had to sing a march or play one on the violin. ...

You will remember that I possess a very good violin which little Wolfgangerl always used to call the butter violin because of its soft, mellow tone. Once, soon after your return from Vienna, he had a go on it and could not find words enough to praise it. A day or two later I came to visit him again and found him about to start amusing himself on his own violin. He immediately said, 'How is your butter violin today?' and carried on extemporizing on his own. After a while he became thoughtful and said, 'Herr Schachtner, your violin is tuned half a quarter-tone lower than mine; if only you would get it tuned as it was when I last played on it.' I laughed, but his father, who knew the boy's extraordinary aural memory and sense of pitch, asked me to fetch my violin to see if he was right. I did so, and he was indeed right. ...

Just after your return from Vienna [in 1763], from where Wolfgang had brought back a little violin he had been given, the late Herr Wenzl brought round six trios which he had written during your father's absence. Herr Wenzl was one of the outstanding violinists of the time who was just starting off as a composer, and he wanted your father's opinion. We played these trios, with your father playing the bass part on his viola, Herr Wenzl playing first violin and myself second. Little Wolfgangerl asked if he could play second violin, but his father dismissed his request as ridiculous, for the boy had no idea about violin playing and his father thought he would be quite incapable of it. Wolfgang said: 'You don't need to have learnt if you're playing second.' His father ordered him to leave the room and stop disturbing us. Wolfgang burst out sobbing and moved towards the door carrying his violin, dragging his feet. I asked for him to be allowed to play along with me: at length his father said: 'Play with Herr Schachtner, but very quietly so that no one can hear you – otherwise, out you go!' So Wolfgang played with me. Soon I realized with astonishment that I was quite superfluous. I laid down my violin and looked at your father. While this was going on, tears of admiration and dawning expectation were running down his cheeks. And so Wolfgang played all the trios. When we had come to the end, Wolfgang was sufficiently emboldened by our admiration to assert that he could even play first violin. We tried this out just for fun, and were convulsed with mirth, for though he played it with utterly wrong, haphazard technique, he never quite had to give up.

Finally, a word about the acuteness and sensitivity of his ear. Until he was nearly ten he had an uncontrollable terror of the trumpet when played alone, without other instruments; if anyone so much as showed him a trumpet it was like holding a loaded pistol to his heart. His father wished to rid him of this childish fear and ordered me to blow a trumpet at him regardless of his entreaties, but, my goodness, I wish I had not allowed myself to be persuaded to do so, for hardly had little Wolfgangerl heard the first blaring note than he turned pale and began to fall to the floor; if I had continued, he would certainly have gone into convulsions.

Andreas Schachtner
letter to Maria Anna Mozart
in *Mozart. Briefe und Aufzeichnungen,*
IV, 1962

The same astonishment at Wolfgang's precociousness is found in the 'Literary Correspondence' of Baron Grimm, Mozart's patron and admirer in Paris.

1 December 1763
Real prodigies are so rare that when they do appear, everyone talks about them. A Kapellmeister from Salzburg called Mozart has just arrived here with two delightful-looking children. His daughter, aged eleven, plays the harpsichord quite brilliantly; she executes the longest, most difficult pieces with astounding precision. Her brother, who will be seven in January, is a phenomenon so extraordinary that one can scarcely believe one's eyes and ears. This child thinks nothing of performing the most difficult pieces with perfect accuracy with hands that can hardly stretch a sixth. What is quite incredible is to see him playing extempore for an hour at a time, abandoning himself to his own inspiration and to a wealth of ravishing ideas which he has no trouble in stringing together with taste and clarity. ...

He thinks nothing of deciphering anything you put before him: he writes and composes with marvellous facility, without needing to go to the harpsichord to find the chords. ... You will guess that he has no difficulty in playing any piece you give him in a different key and in any time-signature you specify; but I have seen something else no less incredible. The other day a lady asked him if he would accompany her by ear, without seeing the music, in an Italian cavatina which she knew by heart; and she began to sing. The child tried out a bass which was not absolutely right, because it is impossible to prepare the accompaniment of a song that one does not know; but when the song was over he asked her to sing it again, and this time he not only played the melody with the right hand but added the bass with the left without hesitation. After this he asked her to sing it ten more times and changed the style of his accompaniment each time;

N o. 180 Ebury Street, where the Mozart family stayed in 1764 during their London visit.

Daines Barrington (1727-1800), an English lawyer and antiquary, writing to the Secretary of the Royal Society, gives the following account of the boy Mozart, having seen him in London in June 1765.

Sir,

If I was to send you a well-attested account of a boy who measured seven feet in height, when he was not more than eight years of age, it might be considered as not undeserving the notice of the Royal Society.

The instance which I now desire you will communicate to that learned body, of as early an exertion of most extraordinary musical talents, seems perhaps equally to claim their attention. ...

Having been informed...that he was often visited with musical ideas, to which, even in the midst of the night, he would give utterance on his harpsichord; I told his father that I should be glad to hear some of his extemporary flights.

The father shook his head at this, saying, that it depended entirely upon his being as it were musically inspired, but that I might ask him whether he was in humour for such a composition.

Happening to know that little Mozart was much taken notice of by Manzoli, the famous singer, who came over to England in 1764, I said to the boy, that I should be glad to hear an extempore *Love Song*, such as his friend Manzoli might choose in an opera.

The boy on this (who continued to sit at his harpsichord) looked back with much archness and immediately began five or six lines of a jargon recitative proper to introduce a love song. He played a symphony which might

he would have done it twenty times if he had not been asked to stop. ...

Monsieur Mozart's children have earned the admiration of everyone who has seen them. The Emperor and Empress overwhelmed them with kindness and they were given the same reception at the courts of Munich and Mannheim. It is a pity that people are so ignorant on musical matters here in France. The father intends to proceed to England and to bring his children back via southern Germany.

Friedrich Melchior von Grimm
Correspondance littéraire, 1763
(published 1877–82)

correspond with an air composed to the single word, *Affetto*. It had a first and second part, which, together with the symphonies, was of the length that opera songs generally last: if this extemporary composition was not amazingly capital, yet it was really above mediocrity, and shewed most extraordinary readiness of invention.

Finding that he was in humour, and as it were inspired, I then desired him to compose a *Song of Rage*, such as might be proper to the opera stage. The boy again looked back with much archness, and began five or six lines of a jargon recitative proper to precede a *Song of Anger*. This lasted also about the same time with the *Song of Love*; and in the middle of it he had worked himself up to such a pitch, that he beat his harpsichord like a person possessed, rising sometimes in his chair. The word he pitched upon for this second extemporary composition was, *Perfido*.

After this he played a difficult lesson, which he had finished a day or two before; his execution was amazing, considering that his little fingers could scarcely reach a sixth on the harpsichord.

His astonishing readiness, however, did not arise merely from great practice; he had a thorough knowledge of the fundamental principles of composition, as, upon producing a treble, he immediately wrote a bass under it, which, when tried, had a very good effect.

He was also a great master of modulation, and his transitions from one key to another were excessively natural and judicious; he practised in this manner for a considerable time with a handkerchief over the keys of the harpsichord.

The facts which I have been mentioning, I was myself an eye-witness of; to which I must add, that I have been informed by two or three able musicians, when [Johann Christian] Bach the celebrated composer had begun a fugue and left off abruptly, that little Mozart hath immediately taken it up, and worked it after a most masterly manner.

Witness as I was myself of most of these extraordinary facts, I must own that I could not help suspecting his father imposed with regard to the real age of the boy, though he had not only a most childish appearance, but likewise had all the actions of that stage of life. For example, whilst he was playing to me, a favourite cat came in, upon which he immediately left his harpsichord, nor could we bring him back for a considerable time. He would also sometimes run about the room with a stick between his legs by way of horse. …

Daines Barrington
in *Philosophical Transactions*, LX, 1770

The description of Mozart by his sister-in-law Sophie Haibel (1763–1846) is recorded in the first biography of him, by Georg Nikolaus Nissen, Constanze Mozart's second husband.

He was always good-humoured, but even in the best of moods he was still pensive. He would look you keenly in the eye and give a thoughtful answer to anything you said, whether serious or light-hearted, yet he always seemed to be deeply preoccupied with something quite different. Even while washing his hands in the morning he would be pacing restlessly up and down the room, his mind working hard. At table he would often take a corner of his napkin, screw it up tightly and rub it around under his nose without seeming to be aware what he was doing. ... In his lighter moments he was keenly interested in each new pastime, for instance riding or billiards. ... His hands and feet were in constant motion; he was always fingering something or other – his hat, pockets, watch-chain, tables, chairs – as if he were playing on a keyboard.

The next three passages are also taken from Nissen's biography.

His hearing was so highly developed and he could discern differences in pitch with such perfect accuracy that he could detect minute flaws in intonation even in the largest orchestra and could identify which player or instrument was the culprit. Then this man, normally so gentle and good-humoured, would fly into a passion and express himself with the utmost vehemence.

It is known that he once unconsciously got up from the piano in the middle of a recital and walked out on his audience because they were not paying attention. He was often criticized for doing this; but unjustly so. Everything he played he felt to the depth of his being: he was all emotion and concentration: how then could he remain in this state if faced with cool indifference or inattention, let alone intrusive chatting?

Throughout his life it was frequently said of him – more in an uncomprehending sort of praise than in criticism or mockery – that all his works, even the most beautiful, were just hurriedly tossed off. It is true that Mozart did not like writing. ... He had to be made, even forced, to do it. But once he had been induced to do it and had warmed to the task, it went very quickly. At least in his latter years, he could compose with such intense concentration of all his mental powers that he seldom had to make any improvements afterwards. Because of this, it could not be said that he wrote as quickly and easily as if it were a trivial occupation; what he wrote had seldom just occurred to him at the time of writing. This was even less the case regarding the general conception and overall structure of the piece in question.

Whether he was alone, or with his wife, or with other people (provided they placed no constraints on him), and particularly during his many journeys by carriage, Mozart had the habit of giving free rein to his imagination to invent new melodies, at the same time occupying his intellect and emotions with arranging, developing and exploiting the new material. In the process he would often hum or even sing aloud, without realizing; he would become burning hot and would brook no disturbance. In this way he completed whole compositions in his head and carried them around with him until he was persuaded to write them down or until he felt the compulsion to get them off his mind. So of course the actual writing process was swift; in fact, while writing the music out he liked it if people around him were idly chatting, and he would even add the occasional word to the conversation.

On his travels he came to the home of X, whose twelve-year-old son was showing great promise on the keyboard. 'Herr Kapellmeister,' said the boy, 'I should like to compose something. How do I start?'

'Don't do anything, anything at all. You must wait.'

'But you were composing when you were younger than I am now.'

'But I didn't ask! If you have the urge to do it, it compels you and torments you; you *have* to do it, and you do, without asking.'

The boy stood abashed and crestfallen as Mozart unleashed this stream of words, and finally said, 'I only meant that perhaps you could recommend me a book so that I could learn the proper way to do it.'

'Look,' Mozart replied more gently, stroking the boy's cheek, 'none of that matters. Here, here and here (pointing to his ears, forehead and heart) – that's where your textbook is. If you have it right in there, then by all means take up your pen, and once you have your composition on paper, you can ask some informed person for an opinion.'

Georg Nikolaus Nissen
Biographie W. A. Mozarts, 1828

Mozart's stay in Paris in 1778 was not a success. Baron Grimm, his mentor, wrote to Leopold to advise against his son's staying any longer.

… He is too trusting, too inactive, too easy to catch, too little concerned about the means which could lead to fortune. In order to get on here it is best to be artful, bold and enterprising; for his own good I wish he had half his talent and twice his acumen, then I would not worry about him. …

Friedrich Melchior von Grimm
letter to Leopold Mozart, 27 July 1778

The young Irish tenor Michael Kelly (1762–1826) became a friend of Mozart in Vienna in the mid-1780s, creating the parts of Don Basilio and Don Curzio in 'The Marriage of Figaro'.

At the period I speak of, the Court of Vienna was, perhaps, the most brilliant in Europe. … All ranks of society were dotingly fond of music, and most of them perfectly understood the science. …

I went one evening to a concert of the celebrated Kozeluch's, a great composer for the piano-forte, and…was there introduced to that prodigy of genius – Mozart. He favoured the company by performing fantasias and capriccios on the pianoforte. His feeling, the rapidity of his fingers, the great execution and strength of his left hand, particularly, and the apparent inspiration of his modulations, astounded me. After this splendid performance we sat down to supper, and I had the pleasure to be placed at table between him and his wife, Madame Constanze Weber, a German lady of whom he was passionately fond. … He conversed with me a good deal about Thomas Linley, the first Mrs. Sheridan's brother, with whom he was intimate at Florence, and spoke of him with great affection. He said that Linley was a true genius, and he felt that, had he lived, he would have been one of the greatest ornaments of the musical world. After supper the young branches of our host had a dance, and Mozart joined them. Madame Mozart told me, that great as his genius was, he was an enthusiast in dancing, and often said that his taste lay in that art, rather than in music.

Michael Kelly.

He was a remarkably small man, very
thin and pale, with a profusion of fine
fair hair, of which he was rather vain.
He gave me a cordial invitation to his
house, of which I availed myself, and
passed a great part of my time there.
He always received me with kindness
and hospitality. – He was remarkably
fond of punch, of which beverage I
have seen him take copious draughts.
He was also fond of billiards, and had
an excellent billiard table in his house.
Many and many a game have I played
with him, but always came off second
best. He gave Sunday concerts, at
which, I never was missing. He was
kind-hearted, and always ready to
oblige, but so very particular, when he
played, that, if the slightest noise were
made, he instantly left off. …

I called on him one evening; he said
to me, 'I have just finished a little duet
for my opera, you shall hear it.' He sat
down to the piano, and we sang it. I
was delighted with it, and the musical
world will give me credit for being so,
when I mention the duet, sung by
Count Almaviva and Susan, 'Crudel
perchè finora farmi languire così'. A
more delicious morceau never was
penned by man, and it has often been
a source of pleasure to me, to have
been the first who heard it, and to have
sung it with its greatly gifted composer.
I remember at the first rehearsal of the
full band, Mozart was on the stage
with his crimson pelisse and gold-laced
cocked hat, giving the time of the
music to the orchestra. Figaro's song,
'Non più andrai, farfallone amoroso',
Bennuci [sic] gave, with the greatest
animation, and power of voice.

I was standing close to Mozart, who,
sotto voce, was repeating, Bravo! Bravo!
Bennuci; and when Bennuci came to
the fine passage, 'Cherubino, alla
vittoria, alla gloria militar', … the
effect was electricity itself, for the whole
of the performers on the stage, and
those in the orchestra, as if actuated by
one feeling of delight, vociferated
Bravo! Bravo! Maestro. Viva, viva,
grande Mozart. Those in the orchestra
I thought would never have ceased
applauding, by beating the bows of
their violins against the music desks.
The little man acknowledged, by
repeated obeisances, his thanks for the
distinguished mark of enthusiastic
applause bestowed upon him.

Michael Kelly
Reminiscences, 1826

Mozart and Freemasonry

Mozart was twenty-eight when he became a Freemason. During the latter part of his life his fellow-Masons proved to be an invaluable source of intellectual, material and moral support.

Much ink has been spilt over Mozart's links with Freemasonry. It was on 14 December 1784 that he was initiated into the Apprentice degree at the Viennese lodge 'Zur Wohlthätigkeit' ('Beneficence'), whose Grand Master was Baron Otto von Gemmingen-Hornberg, whom Mozart had met in Mannheim early in 1778 just before leaving for Paris. The Baron, a writer who admired and translated Shakespeare as well as the 18th-century French authors Rousseau and Diderot, was instrumental in giving Mozart his first introduction to the Masonic Craft. It was probably due to his intervention and that of Count Karl Heinrich

Title page of the score of the cantata *Die Maurerfreude* ('The Masons' Joy'), Vienna 1785.

Joseph von Sickingen, the Elector Palatine's minister in Paris, that Mozart was introduced in Paris to another composer who was also a Mason, François Joseph Gossec. During Mozart's second stay in Mannheim at the end of 1778 von Gemmingen is thought to have suggested a project for an opera based on Voltaire's play *Semiramis*, to a libretto by the Baron himself.

The first Masonic lodge was founded in London on 24 June 1717, under the protection of St John the Baptist, and the movement grew rapidly in Europe and also in America. Its introduction into Germany was effected by Francis of Lorraine (the future Emperor Francis I, who married Maria Theresa in 1736) after his own initiation in 1731. Despite a papal bull in 1738 condemning it, Freemasonry was tolerated and then openly accepted, and the first Viennese lodge opened in 1742. In 1780 Maria Theresa was succeeded by her son Joseph II, with whom she had been sharing power since 1765. There was some hostility to the movement, and by 1786 there were only two lodges left in Vienna. Mozart's lodge had merged with others to form one of these, 'Zur neugekrönten Hoffnung' ('New Crowned Hope').

It is not always realized just how perfect a meeting-point the Masonic order provided for the intellectual élite of an age which was prey to a host of moral and spiritual doubts and questions to which the Church, preoccupied as it was with its political and social role, had no answer. Inspired by traditions derived from mediaeval corporatism (those of the architects and masons, hence the movement's name), and from initiation rites believed to go back to ancient Egypt, Freemasonry adopted the humanist ideals of the Age of Enlightenment which transcended religious dogma. These generous ideals were directed towards human happiness (they were not dissimilar, in fact, to those which led to the French Revolution), and it is not surprising that the sensitive Mozart was attracted by them.

He had had contact with Masons very early: in 1767 in Vienna he composed the song *An die Freude* ('To Joy') to a Masonic text as a token of thanks to the doctor who had looked after him during a smallpox epidemic. Several others influenced his life on the path towards initiation: Dr Mesmer, Gebler (librettist of *Thamos*), von Gemmingen, Le Gros (director of the Concerts Spirituels in Paris), van Swieten, and the mineralogist Ignaz von Born. Mozart progressed rapidly to the Fellow Craft degree, on 7 January 1785, and to Master shortly afterwards. Joseph Haydn was initiated in the same lodge on 11 February and Leopold Mozart on 6 April. It may well have been Mozart's enthusiasm that persuaded them to take this step.

In *Thamos, King of Egypt* (1773), the priests of the sun are a transparently obvious representation of Freemasons benefiting from the Enlightenment; *The Magic Flute* is often considered a testament to the Masonic movement. The line of progress between the two is direct and logical, confirming that Mozart's involvement with Freemasonry was the result of a progressive process of maturing and not just a sudden and temporary whim.

Michel Parouty

Mozart's operas

Three operatic traditions were current in Mozart's day: 'opera buffa' (comic), 'opera seria' (tragic or serious) and the German 'Singspiel', where the dialogue between arias was spoken and not sung as recitative. Mozart composed seventeen operas, in which all three genres are represented. The best of them are amongst the pinnacles of musical achievement.

THE MARRIAGE OF FIGARO

Dramma giocoso in four acts

Count Almaviva
The Countess, his wife
Susanna, her maid
Figaro, the Count's manservant
Cherubino, the Count's page
Marcellina, the Countess's duenna
Don Bartolo, a physician in Seville
Don Basilio, a music master
Don Curzio, a lawyer
Antonio, the chief gardener
Barbarina, his daughter

Act I
In the castle of Aguas-Frescas, Figaro and Susanna are about to be married; Figaro is measuring the room which they have been allocated while Susanna tries on her new hat. She is disturbed to find how near the room is to the apartments of the Count, who has his eye on her and may exercise the *droit de seigneur*. Figaro vows to thwart him.

Marcellina is scheming with Bartolo; Figaro has been unwise enough to sign a declaration of debt promising to marry her if he cannot pay it off, and she intends to hold him to his promise. Cherubino confides in Susanna that he is thrown into turmoil by any feminine presence, and asks her to intercede on his behalf with the Countess to prevent him from being banished from the castle for having been too forward with the gardener's daughter.

The Count enters and begins to pay court to Susanna. Cherubino hides

Susanna (Lucia Vestrio) and Figaro (Giuseppe Naldi) in a London production of *The Marriage of Figaro*, 1817.

behind a large armchair, but the arrival of the music master Basilio forces the Count to hide there too, and Cherubino has only the time to jump into the chair, which Susanna quickly drapes with a dress of the Countess's. The page is soon discovered and the Count, hearing from Basilio that he has a penchant for the Countess, promptly makes arrangements to get rid of him: he will be made an officer and sent off to battle. Figaro teases him in a famous aria.

Act II

The Countess, alone, sings of her grief that the Count no longer loves her. Figaro enters and suggests a plan to make him jealous: he has had delivered to the Count a note alluding to an assignation made by the Countess. Susanna will feign to accept a secret rendezvous with the Count but in fact it will be Cherubino in disguise who actually turns up. The two women amuse themselves planning how to dress Cherubino up as a woman, but while Susanna is off stage looking for a dress, the Count enters. The Countess just has time to bundle the page into an adjoining room, which she locks. The Count, hearing noises, asks questions. The Countess replies that it is Susanna in the next room. The Count decides to force the door and, taking his wife with him, goes to look for tools. Susanna, having returned meanwhile, lets Cherubino out of the anteroom and takes his place. When the Count opens the door, it really is Susanna who emerges, much to everyone's astonishment. Unfortunately the gardener, Antonio, saw someone leaping from the window. Figaro claims that it was he, not the page. Marcellina

chooses this moment to demand her due for the unpaid debt. All this postpones the wedding of Figaro and Susanna.

Act III

Susanna had pretended to accept the Count's rendezvous, but he is suspicious. Meanwhile, in a coup de théâtre, Marcellina and Bartolo have discovered that Figaro is their son, kidnapped as a child by brigands. Marcellina drops her previous idea and another marriage is in prospect as Bartolo declares his intention of marrying her.

Without saying anything to Figaro, the Countess helps Susanna to write a note to the Count arranging the time for the rendezvous. A group of young peasants arrives bringing flowers for the Countess; amongst them is Cherubino, who is quickly unmasked. Barbarina, the gardener's daughter, springs to his defence. At last the marriage is performed, during which Susanna slips the Count the note. The pin with which it is fastened is to be the sign of acceptance.

Act IV

Night has fallen. Figaro comes upon Barbarina, who is searching for the pin which she has been given to deliver to Susanna from the Count. Furious, Figaro inveighs against the female sex, and posts Basilio, Bartolo and some servants in the garden to prove his wife's infidelity. Susanna, who has overheard everything, plans to provoke his jealousy further. She and the Countess have exchanged clothes. Cherubino arrives. In the dark, there is a great confusion of mistaken identities. The Count calls his servants, angry at his supposed betrayal by his wife, but the Countess then appears; he is deeply confused and discomfited. She pardons him, and the 'mad day' ends with general rejoicing.

First performance
Burgtheater, Vienna, 1 May 1786
Nancy Storace (Susanna), Francesco Benucci (Figaro), Luisa Laschi-Mombelli (Countess), Stefano Mandini (Count), Michael Kelly (Don Basilio and Don Curzio), Francesco Bussani (Don Bartolo), Maria Mandini (Marcellina), Dorotea Sardi-Bussani (Cherubino)
Conducted by the composer
First London performance
Pantheon, 2 May 1812

Lorenzo Da Ponte, librettist of 'The Marriage of Figaro', 'Don Giovanni' and 'Così fan tutte', tells how the libretto for 'Figaro' came into being.

I went to Mozart and...asked him if he would like to compose the music for a play I would write for him.

'I would do so most willingly,' he answered at once, 'but I'm sure I shan't get it accepted.'

'I'll see to that', I replied.

... The greatness of his genius demanded a subject which should be ample, elevated and abounding in character and incident. When we were talking about it one day, he asked me if I could easily adapt Beaumarchais' comedy, 'The Marriage of Figaro'. The proposal pleased me very well, and I promised to do as he wished. But there was a great difficulty to be overcome. Only a few days before, the Emperor had forbidden the company at the German theatre to act this same

Lorenzo Da Ponte (1749-1838), librettist of *The Marriage of Figaro, Don Giovanni* and *Così fan tutte*.

comedy, as it was, he said, too outspoken for a polite audience. How could one now suggest it to him for an opera? Baron Wetzlar very generously offered to give me a very fair sum for the words and to have the opera produced in London or in France if it could not be done at Vienna. But I declined his offers and proposed that words and music should be written secretly and that we should await a favourable opportunity to show it to the theatrical managers or to the Emperor, which I boldly undertook to do. Martini was the only one to whom I told our great secret, and out of his regard for Mozart he very readily agreed to my postponing writing for him until I had finished 'Figaro'.

So I set to work, and as I wrote the words he composed the music for them. In six weeks all was ready. As Mozart's good luck would have it, they were in need of a new work at the theatre. So I seized the opportunity and without saying anything to anybody, I went to the Emperor himself and offered him 'Figaro'.

'What!' he said, 'Don't you know that Mozart, though excellent at instrumental music, has only written one opera, and that nothing very great?'

'Without Your Majesty's favour,' I answered humbly, 'I too should have written only one play in Vienna.'

'That is true,' he replied, 'but I've forbidden this "Marriage of Figaro" to the German company.'

'Yes,' I said, 'but as I was writing a play to be set to music and not a comedy, I have had to leave out a good many scenes and shorten a great many more, and I've left out and shortened whatever might offend the refinement and decorum of an entertainment at which Your Majesty presides. And as for the music, as far as I can judge it is extraordinarily fine.'

'Very well,' he answered, 'if that is so, I'll trust your taste as to the music, and your discretion as to the morals. Have the score sent to the copyist.'

I hastened at once to Mozart and had not finished telling him the good news when one of the Emperor's lackeys came with a note requesting him to go to the palace at once with the score. He obeyed the royal command and had various pieces performed before the Emperor, who liked them wonderfully well and was, without exaggeration, amazed by them. He had excellent taste in music, as indeed in all the fine arts, and the great success which this piece achieved throughout the world showed clearly that he was not mistaken in his judgement. ...

A certain Bussani, the stage-manager and costume-keeper, who knew something of every profession except

that of a gentleman, hearing that I had introduced a ballet into 'Figaro', ran at once to the Count [Saur, Chief of Police] and in surprised and disapproving tones said to him, 'Your Excellency, the poet has introduced a ballet into his opera.' The Count immediately sent for me and angrily began the following dialogue. ...

'So the Signor poet has introduced a ballet into "Figaro"?'

'Yes, Your Excellency.'

'Doesn't the Signor poet know that the Emperor won't have ballets in his theatre?'

'No, Your Excellency.'

'Well, Signor poet, I tell you so now.'

'Yes, Your Excellency.'

'And what is more, I tell you you must take it out, Signor poet.'

(This 'Signor poet' was repeated in a significant tone as though he meant 'Signor ass' or something like it, but my 'Excellency' too had its due meaning.)

'No, Your Excellency.'

'Have you the libretto with you?'

'Yes, Your Excellency.'

'Where is the ballet scene?'

'Here, Your Excellency.'

'Well, this is what we do with it.' And so saying, he took out two sheets of my play, threw them quietly on the fire and handed me back the libretto, saying, 'You see, Signor poet, that I can do everything.' Then he honoured me with a second '*Vade*' ['Go'].

I went at once to Mozart who on hearing the bad news was in despair. He wanted to go off to the Count, give Bussani a thrashing, appeal to the Emperor, recall the score – in truth I had a hard task to calm him. ...

Lorenzo da Ponte
Memoirs, 1828
Translated by L. A. Sheppard, 1929

DON GIOVANNI

Dramma giocoso in two acts

Don Giovanni
Donna Anna
Don Ottavio, her fiancé
The Commendatore, her father
Donna Elvira
Leporello, Don Giovanni's servant
Zerlina, a peasant girl
Masetto, her fiancé
The action takes place in a village in Spain.

Act I
In front of the Commendatore's house Leporello awaits his master, Don Giovanni, grumbling about his conditions of service. Donna Anna, the Commendatore's daughter, comes in indignant pursuit of Don Giovanni, who has attempted to seduce her. Her father challenges Don Giovanni to a duel and is killed. Donna Anna goes to look for help and returns with her betrothed, Don Ottavio; over her father's corpse she demands vengeance.

Still on the lookout for more women to seduce, Don Giovanni finds himself confronted with Donna Elvira, whom he had abandoned. He makes off, leaving Leporello to recite to the appalled Donna Elvira the catalogue of his master's conquests.

During a village wedding Don Giovanni leads the bridegroom, Masetto, away, and then makes overtures to the bride, Zerlina. Elvira intervenes, and soon afterwards Donna

The graveyard scene in the 1789 Mannheim production of *Don Giovanni*, designed by Joseph Quaglio.

Anna and Don Ottavio appear, still searching for the killer of the Commendatore. Don Giovanni (in disguise) volunteers to help them, but Elvira warns them against him. Donna Anna has recognized the assassin's voice and once more calls on Don Ottavio to avenge her father's murder.

Don Giovanni gives a party in his palace. He has invited Zerlina, who has managed to calm Masetto down. Three masked figures present themselves and, invited by Leporello, mingle with the guests. They are Donna Anna, Donna Elvira and Don Ottavio in search of justice. To Masetto's fury, Don Giovanni has still not given up the idea of seducing Zerlina. Masetto and the three masked characters are not taken in. Zerlina screams and Don Giovanni turns on Leporello, pretending he is the culprit, and manages to get away.

Act II
Still hoping to seduce Zerlina, Don Giovanni has exchanged clothes with Leporello. Elvira appears at her balcony and Don Giovanni serenades her; she yields to his charms, but by the time she has descended from the balcony, he has vanished, leaving her with Leporello. Masetto and his friends come to seek out the seducer. Giovanni, still in disguise, sends them off on a false trail and beats up Masetto, who has to be consoled by Zerlina. Threatened by Ottavio and Anna, Leporello confesses to the subterfuge. Ottavio demands justice, but Elvira hopes Giovanni will come to no harm; despite his infidelities she still loves him.

Don Giovanni and Leporello have escaped from their pursuers and find themselves in the graveyard next to the statue of the Commendatore. A spectral voice threatens the libertine, but he defiantly invites the statue to dine with him. Anna has put off her marriage to Don Ottavio. While Don Giovanni is at table, Elvira implores him to mend his ways before it is too late, but he brushes her aside. The statue arrives and invites Don Giovanni to accept a return invitation and shake hands. Giovanni holds out his hand. One last time the statue orders him to repent; Giovanni remains defiant and the statue drags him down to the depths of hell.

Anna, Elvira, Zerlina, Ottavio, Masetto and Leporello are left to point the moral of the story.

First performance
National Theatre, Prague, 29 October 1787
Luigi Bassi (Don Giovanni), Felice Ponziani (Leporello), Giuseppe Lolli (The Commendatore and Masetto), Antonio Baglioni (Don Ottavio), Teresa Saporiti (Donna Anna), Catarina Micelli (Donna Elvira), Teresa Bondini (Zerlina). Conducted by the composer
First London performance
King's Theatre, 12 April 1817 (in English)

'Don Giovanni' is Mozart's supreme masterpiece. Of all his operas this is the one which, with its fundamental ambiguities, provides the richest and most complex account of man's metaphysical uncertainties. Through the power of music and the force of genius, the character of Don Giovanni – Don Juan – becomes not only a theatrical hero but a myth.

The figure of Don Juan fascinated the Romantic writers. In the tale of the same name by the German writer and composer E. T. A. Hoffmann, the narrator goes to the opera and, stimulated by the music and under the influence of punch, he fancies he meets Donna Anna.

... Zerlina is rescued, and in the powerful, stormy finale [to Act I] Don Giovanni, his rapier drawn, advances to confront his enemies. He strikes Don Ottavio's flimsy stage sword from his hand and forces his way to freedom through the assembled crowd of ordinary folk, throwing them all pell-mell into amusing confusion.

Several times I had thought I sensed, close behind me, a soft warm breathing and heard the rustle of a silk dress: this intimated to me the presence of a woman, but, being deeply absorbed in the poetic world which the opera was opening up before me, I paid no attention. Now, when the curtain fell, I turned to see who it was. ... How can I describe my astonishment? Donna Anna, dressed in the same costume that I had just seen her wearing on the stage, was standing behind me, the penetrating gaze of her eloquent eyes fixed on me. I looked at her, speechless; her lips seemed to contract into a slight, ironic smile in which I saw my own foolish face reflected. I felt impelled to speak to her, but, paralysed by amazement or, I might almost say, shock, could not utter a word. At long last, almost involuntarily, these words issued from my mouth: 'How is it possible that you are here?' She immediately replied in pure Tuscan that unless I could speak and understand Italian, she would have to do without the pleasure of conversing with me, since she could not speak any other language.

These sweet words fell on my ears like music. As she spoke, her dark blue eyes became even more expressive and every time they flashed I was suffused with a sudden ardour that set my pulse racing and made me tremble in every fibre of my being.

It was Donna Anna, there was no doubt about it. It never occurred to me to wonder how it was possible for her to be on the stage and in my box at the same time. But sometimes a happy dream can blend the strangest elements, and our faith can understand the supernatural and associate it effortlessly with the so-called natural phenomena; similarly in the presence of this strange and magical woman I fell into a state of quasi-somnambulism which enabled me to discover the secret bond which united me with her so closely that she could not have been separated from me even by appearing on the stage.

As she spoke about Don Giovanni and her own role, it was as if the profundity of this masterpiece were being revealed to me for the first time, and I could see clearly into it and discern the fantastical phenomena of an unknown world. She said that music was her whole life, and that often she felt that by singing she could comprehend many things that were locked in the innermost heart and could not be expressed in words. 'Yes,' she went on, her eyes sparkling and her voice rising, 'but all around me remains cold and dead, and when people clap a difficult roulade or a complicated piece of ornamentation, I feel icy hands clasping my heart! – But you...you understand me: for I know that you too have ventured into the wondrous romantic regions that ring with the heavenly magic of music!'

The climax of *Don Giovanni*, where the statue of the Commendatore appears in response to Don Giovanni's invitation to supper – perhaps the most impressive scene in any opera.

The interval bell sounded: a sudden pallor drained the colour from Donna Anna's face, which wore no make-up. Her hand went to her heart, as if she felt a sudden pain, and she quietly said, 'Unhappy Anna, your most terrible moment is upon you.' Then she vanished from the box. ...

I have succeeded in regaining my equilibrium and now I feel capable, my dear Theodor, of putting into words what I believe to be the true significance of this wonderful masterpiece, which I had not grasped until that moment.

If we look at the libretto simply as a story and without attaching any deeper symbolism to it, it is hard to imagine how Mozart could have created such music for it. A *bon vivant*, immoderately fond of wine and women, impulsively invites to supper the stone statue of an elderly father whom he killed in self-defence – really, this idea is not poetically promising,

nor, to be frank, does such a man deserve to be singled out by the infernal powers to be made an exhibition of in hell. ... Believe me, Theodor! Nature treated Juan as her favourite child, equipped him with everything that brings man close to divinity, raising him above ordinary mortals and distinguishing him from the cheap products turned out by workshops which are no more than a series of zeros, meaningless unless preceded by a number.

Don Juan was destined to vanquish and to dominate. A strong, handsome body and a mind shaped as living proof that the flame of divinity burned within him; a profound sensibility, a quick intelligence. ... But the dreadful consequence of the fall of man was that the devil retains the power to lie in wait for him and to lay snares to catch him, even while he is reaching up towards the infinite heights, thereby proving his divine origins. This conflict between

Elisabeth Schwarzkopf as Donna Elvira and Cesare Siepi as Don Giovanni in the 1954 Salzburg production, conducted by Wilhelm Furtwängler.

divine and demonic powers constitutes the essence of earthly life, while the final victory represents celestial life. Don Juan was fired by the desire to grasp life as his bodily and spiritual constitution demanded, and the constantly burning desire tingling in his veins drove him to seize avidly and continually all the experiences the world could offer, hoping for a satisfaction which always eluded him. … Running from one beautiful woman to the next, enjoying the charms of each with a fervour so intense that it became a destructive intoxication; always believing himself mistaken in his choice, ever hoping to find enduring satisfaction with the ideal woman; it was inevitable that Don Juan would finally admit that life was flat and insipid, and, despising all humanity, turn against the one who, having seemed to be all that was most exalted in life, had caused him the bitterest disillusionment. From then on each act

of possessing a woman was not the satisfaction of desire but an irreverent challenge to Nature and its Creator. … His one aspiration is to raise himself above the limitations of this life, but he does so only to be plunged into the depths of hell…

Two o'clock strikes! I feel a thrilling warm breath near me – I sense the subtle odour of fine Italian perfume which was my first intimation of my neighbour yesterday; I am surrounded by a blissful sensation which I feel can only be expressed in music. A stronger current of air moves across the theatre – the strings of the piano in the orchestra vibrate – Heavens! as from a great distance, borne on the wings of a light-toned orchestra in crescendo, I think I hear Anna's voice: 'Non mi dir, bell'idol mio!'

Unfold, distant undiscovered land of the spirits! – Djinnistan, faery region where the enraptured soul is filled with ineffable, heavenly anguish and inexpressible joy, and finds itself heaped to overflowing with all that was unattainable on earth!

E. T. A. Hoffmann
Fantasies after the Manner of Callot,
1814-15

Charles Gounod (1818–93) revered Mozart above all other composers, but Paul Dukas (1865–1935), like Gounod a composer himself, has perhaps more penetrating observations to make.

Throughout my life the score of *Don Giovanni* has been a continual revelation. It has always seemed to me the embodiment of dramatic and musical perfection. In my view it is a peerless, impeccable work; and this judgment is but the humble expression of my gratitude and veneration for the genius to whom I owe the purest, most enduring joys of my life as a musician and composer. There have been a handful of men in history who seem destined to attain, each in his own sphere, a peak higher than which it is not possible to rise: in sculpture, Phidias; in comedy, Molière. Mozart is one of these and *Don Giovanni* is the peak of his achievement.

Charles Gounod
Mozart's 'Don Juan', 1890

One of the particular characteristics of the musical style of *Don Giovanni*, perhaps the most astonishing of all, is the remarkable sobriety of touch with which Mozart obtains effects of extraordinary intensity. From beginning to end he maintains a concealed current of vibrant expression, allowing it to gather in intensity as the work progresses and finally unleashing it in a torrent when the climax of the action calls for it. Musically speaking, the catastrophe at the end of *Don Giovanni* is the inevitable consequence of the tragic situations which have been building up to it. All the most turbulent and brilliant episodes of the score have lurking within them the hidden threat of the final terrible explosion.

It is interesting to note that Madame de Staël, who held the somewhat unusual opinion that Mozart was ingenious rather than a genius, nevertheless appreciated this duality in the musical expression of *Don Giovanni*. In her book *De l'Allemagne* she writes: 'Of all composers it was perhaps Mozart who showed the greatest aptitude and talent for marrying the music to the words. In his operas, especially *Don Giovanni*, he exploits every gradation of drama; the singing is full of gaiety, while the strange, powerful accompaniment seems to reflect the work's sombre symbolism.' However, she then modifies this excellent *aperçu* by adding: 'This spiritual alliance between composer and poet does give pleasure of a kind, but it is a pleasure which is born of reflection and, as such, does not belong within the marvel-filled sphere of the arts.' This is very like what people were later to say of Wagner.

Paul Dukas
Writings on Music, 1948

COSÌ FAN TUTTE

Dramma giocoso in two acts

Fiordiligi, a lady of Ferrara
Dorabella, her sister
Despina, their chamber-maid
Ferrando, in love with Dorabella
Guglielmo, in love with Fiordiligi
Don Alfonso, an old philosopher
The action takes place in Naples.

Act I
In a café Don Alfonso is discussing with his friends Guglielmo and Ferrando the question of women's fidelity. The two young men are confident of their fiancées, Fiordiligi and Dorabella, but Don Alfonso suggests they should be put to the test. With the help of their servant Despina he announces to the two young ladies that their lovers have to leave immediately for the war. Distraught, they tenderly bid them adieu. Scarcely have the young men left than Don Alfonso produces two young Albanians,

who lose no time in declaring their love, but the two sisters repulse them indignantly – each having failed to recognize that the young man wooing her is her sister's lover in disguise. Ferrando and Guglielmo pretend to take poison in despair; Despina, disguised as a doctor, 'revives' them. It is clear that the sisters are not unmoved.

Act II
Encouraged by Despina, the 'Albanians' try their luck again. This time Dorabella agrees to exchange the medallion which Ferrando had given her for a pendant offered by the disguised Guglielmo. Fiordiligi resists longer. Ferrando is hurt by his friend's success with Dorabella and becomes convinced of the fickleness of women. More and more distressed, and persuasively urged by Despina and Alfonso to accept Ferrando, Fiordiligi thinks of going to join her fiancé on the battlefield. But, won over by the feigned despair of Ferrando, she gives in to him – to the fury of Guglielmo, observing from a hiding-place.

The two young men resolve to break their engagements, but Don Alfonso convinces them that all women behave in the same way ('Così fan tutte').

At dinner the two newly-formed couples drink a toast to their love. Despina, disguised as a notary, arrives to perform a marriage ceremony, but at that moment trumpets are heard off-stage announcing the return of the armies. The 'Albanians' quickly leave; Ferrando and Guglielmo make their entry and appear astonished to get such a luke-warm reception. All is revealed when Ferrando demands to see his medallion and Guglielmo's pendant is found on Dorabella. Despina removes her mask and the sisters discover that they have been duped. The couples form up again as at the start, but with no illusions.

First performance
Burgtheater, Vienna, 26 January 1790
Vincenzo Calvesi (Ferrando), Francesco Benucci (Guglielmo), Francesco Bussani (Don Alfonso), Adriana Ferrarese (Fiordiligi), Louise Villeneuve (Dorabella), Dorotea Sardi-Bussani (Despina)
Conducted by the composer
First London performance
Haymarket Theatre, 9 May 1811

The English conductor Sir Thomas Beecham (1879–1961), whose recorded performances of Mozart operas are still prized today, relates the story of his revival of 'Così fan tutte' in London in 1910.

I then took in hand a short Mozart cycle. … *Così fan tutte* proved easily the most interesting; few had ever heard of it, and fewer still seemed acquainted with the music, although it is equal in beauty to anything the composer ever wrote. As one lovely melody followed another until it seemed as if the invention of Mozart was inexhaustible, the whole culminating in the wonderful canon-quartette of the last scene, it was hard to believe that in our age of vaunted culture and education a work like this, then one hundred and twenty years old, was being heard almost for the first time in a great city like London. Admittedly it lacks the breadth and dramatic poignancy of *Don Giovanni*, the brilliant and acute vigour of *Figaro*, or the bright dewy freshness of *Il Seraglio*: nor do we find

Ferrando, disguised as an Albanian, with Fiordiligi (Kiri te Kanawa) in the 1976 Paris production of *Così fan tutte*.

there any of those solemn intimations which are heard now and then in *Die Zauberflöte*. *Così fan tutte* is a long summer day spent in a cloudless land by a Southern sea. ... In *Così fan tutte* the dying eighteenth century casts a backward glance over a period outstanding in European life for grace and charm and, averting its eyes from the view of a new age suckled in a creed of iconoclasm, sings its swan-song in praise of a civilization that has passed away for ever.

Sir Thomas Beecham
A Mingled Chime, 1944

It should not be concluded that the music becomes more sincere as the characters drop their pretences. Mozart is as direct – and as pretentious – in the one instance as in the other. The irony of the opera depends on its tact; it is a masterpiece of 'tone', this most civilized of all aesthetic qualities. There is no way of knowing in what proportions mockery and sympathy are blended in Mozart's music and how seriously he took his puppets. ... Even to ask is to miss the point: the art in these matters is to tell one's story without being foolishly taken in by it and yet without a trace of disdain for its apparent simplicity. ... Those who think that Mozart wrote profound music for a trivial libretto misunderstand his achievement. ... The farewell quintet in the first act is a touchstone of Mozart's success: heartbreaking without ever for a moment approaching tragedy, and delightful without a trace of explicit mockery in the music, it seems to hold laughter and sympathy in a beautiful equilibrium.

Charles Rosen
The Classical Style, 1971

THE MAGIC FLUTE

Singspiel in two acts

Sarastro, Priest of the Sun
Tamino, a foreign prince
Speaker
The Queen of the Night
Pamina, her daughter
Three Ladies
Three Boys
Papageno, a bird-catcher
Papagena
Monostatos, a Moor

Act I
Pursued by a serpent, Prince Tamino is saved by three ladies – not by Papageno, who attempts to take the credit. When Tamino recovers from his faint, they give him a portrait of Pamina, the daughter of their Queen, held prisoner by Sarastro. To punish Papageno for his lies they padlock his mouth. The Queen of the Night appears and promises Tamino her daughter's hand in marriage if he can rescue her. The ladies remove Papageno's padlock, give him a set of bells, and provide Tamino with a magic flute to protect him.

In Sarastro's palace Monostatos is pestering Pamina, but Papageno arrives and chases the Moor away. Meanwhile the three boys have conducted Tamino to the portals of the temples of Nature, Reason and Wisdom. Delighted to know that he will soon meet Pamina, Tamino plays his flute and enchants the wild animals. To escape from the slaves whom Monostatos has sent to catch him, Papageno shakes his bells, and they are enchanted. At this point Sarastro arrives. He comforts Pamina and asks her not to see her mother again. Monostatos appears, followed by Tamino, who has been captured. He and Pamina fall in love at first sight.

Act II
Sarastro prays to Isis and Osiris to grant protection to Tamino and Pamina. The first trial that Tamino and Papageno have to undergo is that of silence. They succeed despite the attempts of the three ladies to make them speak. The Queen of the Night gives her daughter a dagger and orders her to kill Sarastro. Monostatos reappears and threatens to denounce Pamina, but Sarastro intervenes. He reassures the young girl again; it is not his intention to seek vengeance on the Queen of the Night. The trials of Tamino and Papageno continue. An old woman appears before Papageno, saying she is his

T itle page of an early vocal score of *The Magic Flute,* showing Papageno and Tamino with the dead serpent.

Papageno with his birdcage and feather-clad children crown the 'Papageno Portal' of the Theater an der Wien, Vienna, by Franz and Anton Jäger. This theatre, completed in 1801, took over the role of the Theater auf der Wieden, burnt in that year, and saw many performances of *The Magic Flute* as well as other operas by Mozart.

promised bride, Papagena, but disappears again. Tamino, still under the command of silence, is in despair because he cannot speak to Pamina. Papageno finds the old woman again, and she is transformed into a charming girl; but his trials are not yet over and again she disappears.

Pamina, in utter despair, tries to kill herself. She is prevented by three boys, who lead her to Tamino for the final trial, that of fire and water. Papageno, not finding Papagena again, attempts to hang himself, but on the advice of the three boys he shakes his bells again and Papagena reappears.

Monostatos has been persuaded by the Queen of the Night to help him abduct Pamina, but in the face of the Light, the powers of night are

vanquished. Pamina and Tamino, finally united, have found the Truth.

First performance
Theater auf der Wieden, Vienna, 30 September 1791
Franz Xaver Gerl (Sarastro), Benedikt Schak (Tamino), Josepha Weber-Hofer (Queen of the Night), Anna Gottlieb (Pamina), Emanuel Schikaneder (Papageno), Barbara Gerl (Papagena), Johann Joseph Nouseul (Monostatos) Conducted by the composer
First London performance
His Majesty's Theatre (in Italian), 6 June 1811

The origin of *Die Zauberflöte*, like that of the Requiem, is covered with a web of legends. Mozart is supposed to have

The summer-house where Mozart is said to have composed *The Magic Flute*.

rescued Schikaneder, by means of this work, from financial difficulties; Schikaneder is said to have kept him in good humor during its composition by giving him wine and oysters and to have kept him locked up in a garden-house near the theater. This house was brought to the Capuziner-Berg near Salzburg in 1874, as the Santa Casa to Loreto, and every board in it is presumably as authentic as every one in the Santa Casa itself. Mozart is supposed to have hesitated to accept the proposal for fear of a fiasco, for 'he had not yet composed a magic opera'. All this is nonsense, of course. The work was produced on 30 September and its success grew with every repetition. ...

The weakness of the libretto – a small weakness, easily overcome – lies only in the diction. It contains a great number of unskilful, childish, vulgar turns of speech. But the critics who therefore decide that the whole libretto is childish and preposterous deceive themselves. At any rate Goethe did not so consider it when he wrote a *'Zauberflöte* Part II', unfortunately unfinished, but full of fairy-tale radiance, poetic fantasy, and profound thought. In the dramaturgic sense Schikaneder's work is masterly. The dialogue could be shortened and improved, but not a stone in the structure of these two acts and of the work as a whole could be removed or replaced, quite apart from the fact that any change would demolish Mozart's carefully thought out and organic succession of keys. ...

[The plot] seems merely a fantastic entertainment, intended to amuse suburban audiences by means of machines and decorations, a bright and variegated mixture of marvelous events and coarse jests. It is such an entertainment, to a certain extent; but it is much more, or rather it is something quite different, thanks to Mozart. *Die Zauberflöte* is one of those pieces that can enchant a child at the same time that it moves the most worldly of men to tears, and transports the wisest. Each individual and each generation finds something different in it; only to the merely 'cultured' or the pure barbarian does it have nothing to say. Its sensational success with its first audiences in Vienna arose from political reasons, based on the subject-matter. Mozart and Schikaneder were Freemasons; Mozart an enthusiastic one, and Schikaneder surely a crafty and active one. The latter used symbols of Freemasonry quite openly in the libretto. The first edition of the libretto contained something rare in such books – two copperplate engravings, one showing Schikaneder-Papageno in his costume of feathers, but the other showing the portal to the 'inner rooms', the great pyramid with hieroglyphs, and a series of emblems: five-pointed star, square and trowel, hour-glass and overthrown pillars and plinths. Everyone understood this. After a period of tolerance for the 'brothers' under Joseph II, a reaction had set in with Leopold II, and there had begun again secret persecutions and repressions. ... Under the cloak of symbolism *Die Zauberflöte* was a work of rebellion, consolation, and hope. Sarastro and his priests represent hope in the victory of light, of humanity, of the brotherhood of man. Mozart took care, by means of rhythm, melody, and orchestral color, to make the

significance of the opera, an open secret, still clearer. He began and ended the work in E-flat major, the Masonic key. The slow introduction of the Overture begins with the three chords, symbolizing the candidate knocking three times on the portal; and then in the climactic scene Tamino knocks on three different doors. A thrice-played chord follows Sarastro's opening of the ceremonies in the temple. Woodwinds – the typical instruments of the Viennese lodges – play a prominent part; the timbre of the trombones, heretofore used by Mozart – in *Idomeneo*, in *Don Giovanni* – only for dramatic intensification, now takes on symbolic force.

Frontispiece of the first edition of the libretto of *The Magic Flute*.

Emanuel Schikaneder.

These Masonic elements had little meaning for the 'uninitiated' and have had even less for later generations. What remains is the eternal charm of the naive story, the pleasure in Schikaneder's skill…and the wondering awe at Mozart's music. The work is at once childlike and godlike, filled at the same time with the utmost simplicity and the greatest mastery.

Alfred Einstein
Mozart: his Character, his Work
Translated by Arthur Mendel and
Nathan Broder, 1946

The musicologist H. C. Robbins Landon, who has made a special study of Mozart and the Masons, considers the circumstances surrounding the composition of 'The Magic Flute', with its use of the ideals, rituals, and number symbolism of a very secret society.

… it was suggested long ago that the Masons killed Mozart. There are, very simply, two facts which render this theory – which is considered very attractive in some quarters even today – not only unlikely but impossible. The first is that no one killed Schikaneder, who was just as responsible for 'betraying Masonic secrets' as Mozart. … And the second reason is equally, if not more, convincing: Mozart's own Lodge held a Lodge of Sorrows for their composer, printed the main speech, and also printed the Masonic cantata (K.623) Mozart had composed before he died.
… The fact of the matter is that Freemasonry in Austria was in acute danger of extinction. … The reason for this sudden danger in which the Masons found themselves was their supposed involvement with the French Revolution. … In the face of such suspicion and hostility, how was Masonry to be protected? How were its greatness and universality to be presented to the general public? The two Masons, Mozart and Schikaneder, decided to write the first Masonic opera – *The Magic Flute*. Wisely, they treated the whole subject in two ways: with dignity, love and respect – as true Brothers – but also not without humour, with even a hint of malicious satire. … The audience in September 1791 went home with the feeling that the Masons were the embodiment of the Enlightenment – and besides, much of the opera was genuine good fun. …
Mozart obviously found the amazing diversity of the subject immensely

attractive. In the final score, this ranges from the Haydnesque folk-tunes of the music for the 'simple' beings, Papageno and Papagena, to the mystical and ritualistic music for Sarastro and his court, and from the mad coloratura of the Queen of the Night...to the inclusion of an antique-sounding north German Lutheran chorale tune, sung by the two men in armour. It was this same diversity that so impressed Beethoven (who in any case disapproved of Da Ponte's texts for the Italian operas as being too frivolous) and which impresses us, too.

H. C. Robbins Landon
1791: Mozart's Last Year, 1988

In 'Idomeneo' and 'La clemenza di Tito' Mozart contravenes the conventions of 'opera seria' just as he surpasses those of 'opera buffa' in 'Die Entführung aus dem Serail': in all these operas his prime concern is the accurate depiction of human nature.

IDOMENEO, 1781

Idomeneo, king of Crete, returning home after a prolonged absence, is almost drowned in a storm at sea: he vows to sacrifice to Neptune the first living human being he encounters. Alas, this turns out to be his son Idamante. The latter loves Ilia, the Trojan princess, and is loved by Electra, daughter of Agamemnon. Idomeneo wishes to send his son away to protect him, but a sea-monster comes to threaten the Cretans. The monster, an envoy of Neptune, is killed by Idamante. But Idomeneo must keep his vow. Just before the sacrifice is to take place, a divine voice is heard: Idomeneo

is to abdicate in favour of his son, who is to marry Ilia – to Electra's fury. In the general rejoicing Idomeneo celebrates the return of peace.

THE SERAGLIO, 1782

Constanze, engaged to Belmonte, has been captured by pirates with her maid, Blonde, and the latter's fiancé, Pedrillo, Belmonte's valet. They have been taken to the palace of Pasha Selim, where they are being detained. With Pedrillo's aid Belmonte succeeds in tricking the vigilant Osmin, the keeper of the harem, and freeing the prisoners. But they are caught while fleeing. The Pasha turns out to be a former enemy of Belmonte's father, who had once persecuted him; but he is magnanimous and pardons them all.

LA CLEMENZA DI TITO ('The Clemency of Titus'), 1791

The Roman emperor Vitellius has been deposed by Titus. His daughter Vitellia attempts to organize a conspiracy with the help of the patrician Sextus, who is in love with her. The young man, who loves and admires the new emperor, hesitates but finally agrees. Learning that the emperor has resolved to marry her, having renounced both Berenice and Servilia (Sextus' sister), Vitellia tries to forestall the assassination, but too late. It turns out, however, that Sextus had only attacked one of the conspirators. He is arrested and admits his crime but without compromising Vitellia. She is much distressed and confesses to Titus, who, despite his sorrow, grants them all his pardon.

Mozart in the eyes of musicians and critics

The appreciation of Mozart by critics and audiences has varied greatly over the years, though he has never failed to excite the interest and admiration of other musicians, even when out of favour with the general public. He has different things to say to every generation.

Two composers express their views

Where the latter [Beethoven] is obscure and seems to lack unity, the cause is not the supposed rather wild originality for which he is esteemed; it is that he turns his back on eternal principles. Mozart never does this. Each voice in Mozart has its own line which, while according perfectly with the other voices, forms its own melody which it follows in the most perfect manner. That is true counterpoint, *punto contrapunto*.

Frédéric Chopin
in Eugène Delacroix, *Journal*, 1823-54

Music must be set free from any sort of scientific approach; its aim must simply be to *give pleasure*. Within these limits it is possible to achieve great beauty. Extreme complication is the antithesis of art. Beauty must be something that can be *felt*, the pleasure it gives must be immediate; it must impose itself on us, or insinuate its way into us, without our having to make the least effort to reach out towards it. Look at Leonardo, look at Mozart. There were two great artists!

Claude Debussy
Monsieur Croche, 1921

A great French historian responds to Mozart's genius

Even when Mozart is joyous he never ceases to be noble; he is never a *bon vivant*, a simple epicurean like Rossini: he never makes mock of feelings or slips into vulgar joviality. There is a supreme refinement in his gaiety; when he does indulge in it, he does so gradually, by degrees, because his musical personality is flexible and because in any truly great artist no aspect is missing. But at the heart of him is an unconditional love of civilized, serene beauty.

Hippolyte Taine
Life and Opinions of Mr Frédéric Graindorge, 1867

Shaw defends Mozart

At the time of the first centenary of Mozart's death in 1891 he was not fully appreciated by the public. Bernard Shaw, who was a music critic in London before becoming a dramatist, was one of his most fervent champions.

Unfortunately, Mozart's music is not everybody's affair when it comes to conducting it. His scores do not play themselves by their own physical weight, as many heavy modern scores do. When a sense of duty occasionally urges Mr Manns or the Philharmonic to put the G minor or the E flat or the Jupiter Symphony in the bill, the band, seeing nothing before them but easy diatonic scales passages and cadences smoothly turned on dominant discords, races through with the general effect of a couple of Brixton schoolgirls playing one of Diabelli's pianoforte duets. The audience fidgets during the *allegro*; yawns desperately through the *andante*; wakes up for a moment at the minuet, finding the trio rather pretty; sustains itself during the *finale* by looking forward to the end; and finishes by...voting me stark mad when I speak of Mozart as the peer of Bach and Wagner, and, in his highest achievements, the manifest superior of Beethoven.

George Bernard Shaw
'A Mozart Controversy'
The World, 11 June 1890

A conductor considers *The Seraglio*

The great Mozartian Sir Thomas Beecham paid tribute in his autobiography to 'The Seraglio'.

Here at last we find the full-grown and mature Mozart, emancipated from the traditions and conventions of a style of operatic composition that had held the stage for eighty years and of which his *Idomeneo* is a first-rate example. In *Il Seraglio* we are introduced to a new and living world. Gone from the scene are the pallid heroes and heroines of antiquity, the unconvincing wizards and enchantresses of the Middle Ages and all the other artificial creatures dear to the whole tribe of eighteenth century librettists. In their unlamented place we have ordinary human beings of recognizable mould, singing their joy and sorrows to melody that rings as freshly in our ears today as in those of the Viennese one hundred and sixty years ago.

In songs of the highest excellence the score is exceptionally rich. ... But astonishing as is this exhibition of solo virtuosity, it is outrivalled by the ensemble pieces, of which the finale to the second act is the crown. Here we have the first instance on a large scale of that matchless skill with which Mozart could weave together a succession of movements, each representing a different mood or stage in the action, into a complete unity that is entirely satisfying to the musical sense. And as the absolute fitness of the music to the dramatic situation is never in question for a moment, all flows on with a natural ease beyond which human art cannot go. In the last number of all, the Vaudeville, we have a specimen of that haunting strain peculiar to this master, half gay, half sad, like the smile on the face of a departing friend. These tender adieux abound in the later Mozart.

Sir Thomas Beecham
A Mingled Chime, 1944

Mozart becomes the subject of detailed critical analysis

Mozart's way of reaching his listeners is to make use of a faultless technical equipment. His is so smooth and natural a technique as to be very easily overlooked. In fact we are not intended to be made aware of it or to admire it for its own sake: it is merely the means to an end, and in the case of one so supremely gifted a perfectly convenient and untroublesome means, even where it involves appalling difficulties. No parade is ever made of skill or learning. Sometimes, it is true, as in the finale of the *Jupiter Symphony*, sheer pleasure in the exercise of a staggering virtuosity takes hold of Mozart irresistibly; but even there the music remains clear, its surface undisturbed by the polyphonic problems he tackles, so that the hearer who remains unaware of them still enjoys the incomparable flow and polish of the music.

Mozart's sovereign ease in the handling of counterpoint is the very foundation of his style and one of the great differences between him and Beethoven, who happened to find counterpoint difficult – which is not to say that he eschewed it or that, when he faced it, he failed to do justice to his own peculiar genius. What distinguishes Mozart is the fact that he always applied this gift of his, whether he intended to write polyphonically or not, and that, considering how readily contrapuntal writing came to him, he made conscious use of polyphonic skill surprisingly rarely. But it was at the very root of his technique, even where he simply wrote accompanied melody. It is this which explains why his part-writing and his spacing are always, whatever the nature of the musical texture may be at the moment, superbly lucid and limpid.

Eric Blom
in Ralph Hill, *The Symphony*, 1949

In the G minor Symphony [no. 40, K.550], a work of passion, violence, and grief for those who love Mozart most, Schumann saw nothing but lightness, grace, and charm. It should be said at once that to reduce a work to the expression of sentiments, however powerful, is to trivialize it in any case: the G minor Symphony is not much more profound conceived as a tragic cry from the heart than as a work of exquisite charm. Nevertheless, Schumann's attitude to Mozart ends by destroying his vitality as it canonizes him. It is only through recognizing the violence and the sensuality at the center of Mozart's work that we can make a start towards a comprehension of his structures and an insight into his magnificence. ... In all of Mozart's supreme expressions of suffering and terror – the G minor Symphony, *Don Giovanni*, the G minor Quintet [K.516], Pamina's aria in *Die Zauber-flöte* – there is something shockingly voluptuous. Nor does this detract from its power or effectiveness: the grief and the sensuality strengthen each other, and end by becoming

Opening Allegro of Mozart's Sonata for Harpsichord and Violin in B flat major, K.8, composed in Paris when he was seven. The manuscript, in Leopold's hand, is dated 21 November 1763.

indivisible, indistinguishable one from the other.

Charles Rosen
The Classical Style, 1971

A great pianist and two famous sopranos speak from their experience as performers

Artur Schnabel was one of the 20th century's outstanding pianists.

I am attracted only to music which I consider to be better than it can be performed. Therefore I feel (rightly or wrongly) that unless a piece of music presents a problem to me, a never-ending problem, it doesn't interest me too much. For instance, Chopin's studies are lovely pieces, perfect pieces, but I simply can't spend time on them. I believe I know these pieces; but playing a Mozart sonata, I am not sure that I do know it, inside and out.

Therefore I can spend endless time on it. This can probably only be understood by one who has had the same experience. Many colleagues of mine would laugh at me. They would say: 'What is the problem? I don't see any problem.' Here we come to the absolutely uninvestigatable field of *quality* – the demarcation line between quality and quantity, essence and appearance. Once I was asked by somebody: 'How is it that you speak with such reverence and awe of Mozart's profundity?' It was the wife of a star virtuoso to whom I once spoke in almost deliberately exaggerated terms of the depth of Mozart's music, the unfathomable, transcendental qualities. She said: 'We too love Mozart, but we think his music is just sweet and lovely and graceful. If your valuation,' she continued, 'is the right one, Mr Schnabel, how do you explain the fact that all children play Mozart so well?' I answered: 'Well, children have at least one very important element in common with Mozart, namely purity. They are not yet spoiled and prejudiced and personally involved. But these are, of course, not the reasons why their teachers give them Mozart to play. Children are given Mozart because of the small *quantity* of the notes; grown-ups avoid Mozart because of the great *quality* of the notes – which, to be true, is elusive!'

Artur Schnabel
My Life and Music, 1961

Elisabeth Schwarzkopf, one of the foremost Mozart singers of recent times, explains why singing Mozart presents a uniquely rewarding challenge to singers.

Even a naturally frail voice like my own must respond to Mozart's demand for a high degree of vocal deportment and poise. The voice must communicate itself to the audience, but it must also surpass its own standard. Maria Ivogün, my teacher, once said to me, 'Be noble, my dear!' At the time I was working on a Mozart concert aria with violin obbligato. The violin has a magical sonority, a radiance in its legato, which the voice must attempt to imitate. In all his operas Mozart wrote marvellous parts for the wind; the singer must listen attentively to each one and reflect in the voice the different tone-colours which Mozart has put into the orchestra. This is why it's so important for a singer to sing Mozart only in the best possible instrumental environment, and with a real 'ensemble' of singers. With each different partner you find some new aspect or nuance to which you must adapt yourself. It's no use having a lot of vibrato in the voice; it kills Mozart by preventing the voice

E lisabeth Schwarzkopf in the role of Donna Elvira in *Don Giovanni*.

from blending with the instrumental ensemble. But there is no greater pleasure for a singer than to have to adapt in this way. Mozart makes it a privilege. But it also demands *discipline*!

Elisabeth Schwarzkopf
from an interview with André Tubeuf
Le Point, 25 October 1982

The much-loved soprano Irmgard Seefried discusses these challenges further.

When I was a student I didn't realize Mozart would become such an important part of my life; only when I got to Vienna did this become apparent. In 1943 I sang Susanna in *Figaro* and the Composer in *Ariadne auf Naxos* at the State Opera with Karl

Böhm – two roles and two composers who have played a large part in my career. Only later did I realize the importance of Mozart for singing Strauss.

Susanna is a long and difficult role; she is on stage almost all the time, and the success or failure of the whole thing depends on her. To sing Susanna you must be a good actress and have a flawless technique. This applies to any Mozart role, of course.

Naturalness

The singer must be able to sing with naturalness and to move naturally about the stage; the voice and body must be in natural harmony with one another. In reality naturalness can only be the result of a great deal of work. There is no short cut to singing Mozart well. There is no such thing as a Mozartian voice, or a born Mozart singer; you become one after much effort and sacrifice. The Mozart singer is therefore an actor able and willing to undertake endless variations in this combination of voice and body. This is absolutely fundamental, especially for the recitatives, which are so difficult to master – a kind of sung speech or spoken song. It is the recitatives that contain much of the dramatic characterization. There must not be any abrupt break between recitative and aria – it all follows on and you must pass from the one to the other, whether legatissimo or staccato, with complete naturalness – I use that word again. The line can be straight or curved, but it must never be broken. I learnt a lot

Title page of a 19th-century vocal score of *The Marriage of Figaro*.

on this point from the Italians. When we were at La Scala with Karajan it was no joke: the cast was made up of Italians and Germans or Austrians, a difficult and potentially explosive mixture. There was great rivalry. Karajan said, 'I warn you, this will be a flop.' La Scala had its own particular way of singing Mozart. But in the end all went well. The Italians taught me a lot about recitatives, that staccato way of singing *parlando* which is so hard for those born north of the Alps.

The importance of ensemble

To sing Mozart you have to enjoy collaboration. We had a team of singers and orchestral players and used to rehearse together every day. Nowadays this sort of practising no longer happens: singers are usually jetting around and their roles are rehearsed by understudies! And the young ones want to become stars and only sing Mozart *en passant.* ... But that's unwise of them. This teamwork was the strength of Vienna. The conductors, including Böhm and Krips, formed a strong, homogeneous unit with the singers. They worked, thought and rehearsed together, and the result was a uniquely harmonious blend. Performances under Böhm and Krips were pure, clear and perfect. They would not tolerate the slightest sloppiness or approximation – everything always had to be perfect. That's why we had to train so intensively. Italian voices are trained towards producing a big sound, but this is catastrophic for Mozart. Someone once asked a great Italian tenor what he thought of a performance of *Der Rosenkavalier*. He replied, 'Poco voce, poco voce!' (too little voice). Mozart's view of the human voice was quite un-Italian; he disliked any bawling or vocal

I rmgard Seefried as Susanna in *The Marriage of Figaro*.

slovenliness. Mozart must be sung with grace, poise and restraint, with humility and simplicity. It needs discipline like at the Spanish Riding School.

Singing in ensemble does not mean giving up your own personality. It means adding your personality to the total effect. In Mozart the voices are quite interchangeable: the key to it is to find the right colours and intonation to suit each partner. Passage-work is vitally important. The chest voice is dangerous: too much vocal weight is enemy number one, for the voice must remain flexible, malleable and light. Up and down, up and down, *ad libitum*. If you have a big voice you can sing Wagner more or less well, but for Mozart volume is irrelevant – you have to have complete control and be able to sing pianissimo when necessary, and that means you have to practise technique every day – scales, passage-work, breathing, *vocalise*.

A schooling in Mozart is a hard one, but it's the best of all. Armed with this sophisticated technique, which is a different conception of singing, you can tackle any other composer, including modern ones, provided they lie within your vocal range. I'm thinking particularly of the composers of the second Viennese School. An understanding of beautiful *singing* as distinct from a beautiful *sound* is what matters for Mozart – in fact, a succession of beautiful sounds is a guarantee of deadly boredom. To sum up: Mozart is lightness with depth, both tangible and impalpable.

I am a Mozart singer because I have always loved singing Mozart, a composer with whom I have had a privileged relationship. Pamina is probably my favourite role, but I have had immense, intense pleasure from my other roles too. I remember a *Don Giovanni* at Salzburg which was quite unforgettable, with Ljuba Welitsch as a magnificent Donna Anna and Schwarzkopf superb as Elvira. But the whole team – Dermota, Kunz, etc. – was wonderful. Each conductor conducted differently; each had a different vision – Böhm, Krips, Karajan. Furtwängler adored Mozart although it wasn't quite his scene. He had to work hard at it. I remember some very beautiful things conducted by him. Krips enjoyed the musical quality of the ensemble and produced some grandiose finales. Böhm was the one for precision and purity.

All of us worked in the service of Mozart, and after much toil, trial and tribulation we found the immense joy of encountering true genius in him. There were no individual stars. The ensemble itself was the star.

Irmgard Seefried
from an interview with
Christian Schirm
L'Avant-Scène Opéra, October 1985

Instrumental performers give a valuable insight into questions of authenticity in performing Mozart on the piano and violin

If any musician is now interested in gaining a clear idea of the sound of instruments in Mozart's time, he should examine the changes that have taken place in this direction during the past 200 years.

The tonal picture has altered in many respects; the developments of recent centuries have aimed at a greater volume of tone, greater compass, better intonation and, very often, greater ease of performance. ...

In achieving greater volume, the character of piano tone has been steadily altered. It seems that the human ear only reacts favourably to very bright sounds, rich in overtones, when they are not very loud. Forte, these sounds tend to make a sharp, shrill effect, and fortissimo they are almost unbearably strident. So it is not at all surprising that, in comparison with Mozart's piano, even Beethoven's, and *a fortiori* the pianos of the nineteenth and twentieth centuries, have not only a fuller, louder tone, but also one that is darker and usually duller. This was an inevitable development of the manufacture of pianos. Compared with the modern piano, Mozart's piano, with its many overtones, produces an extraordinarily thin, translucent effect, sharply defined and 'silvery'. The instrument was more delicately built, the strings were thinner, and this made its tone relatively weak. The levels of volume to which we are accustomed were impossible until the introduction of the steel frames by A. Balcock in

1825, and the associated increase in string-tension. ...

It should not be supposed that our piano is capable of subtler nuances; the Mozart pianos of Stein and Walter, for instance, were clear and very bright in the upper register, and this made it easier to play cantabile and with full colour. The lower notes had a peculiar round fullness, but none of the dull, stodgy sound of the low notes of a modern piano. Whereas the tone becomes steadily thinner toward the top, the highest register sounding almost as if pizzicato, the full sound of the bass is by far the most satisfying register of the Mozart piano. The strings are so thin that chords in the bass can be played with perfect clarity even when they are closely spaced. On a modern piano such chords usually sound sodden and earthy.

It is certainly true that nowadays we are accustomed to a much greater degree of noise than in earlier times – street noises, the thunder of railways and the roaring of aeroplanes, the stentorian tones of larger-than-life loudspeakers in cinemas and at public gatherings, and enormous orchestras in the concert hall. If we were to recreate the absolute intensity levels of the

Mozart's piano. Built in Vienna by Anton Walter in 1780, it was bought in 1784 by Mozart, who had it fitted with a special sustaining device.

eighteenth century, it is certain that the resulting sound would at first seem much too thin and lacking in penetration. We must reconcile ourselves to the fact that a forte, if it is to sound like one to us, must in acoustical terms be louder than in Mozart's time. For all that, even today a Mozart forte should still not have the volume of tone of a Wagner forte.

A forte, however, is not only an acoustical but a psychological effect. And here it is quite the other way round; in Mozart a forte, though in fact having a smaller degree of loudness, will usually require more psychological intensity than a forte in Wagner, since for Mozart, *forte* may already mean 'full out', whereas in Wagner *f* is only rarely a dynamic climax, in view of his use of dynamics as loud as *fff*.

> Eva and Paul Badura-Skoda
> *Interpreting Mozart on the Keyboard*,
> 1962

Clearly it is the bow which brings the music to life; when the bow ignores the 'breathing' quality of the music as the result of constant pressure, players look for a different way to enliven the performance. During the nineteenth century this task fell to the newly invented *portamento*; our century has adopted the constant vibrato. But both these devices stand in the way of musical clarity: *portamento* covers up the openings in the articulation, while vibrato (when used as a device of tension) destroys the transparent quality of the sound. And a lack of clarity is damaging to the scores of Mozart. ...

One aspect of Mozart interpretation that has been much influenced by the increasing inherent tension of post-classical instruments is the tempo. Playing the classical violin, with its gut strings and with the older, more flexible bow, helps to rediscover a sense of speed that is closely related to the human pulse and does not need extreme values at both ends of the scale. ... Speed must always serve the purpose of the musical discourse if it is not to degenerate into empty brilliance. No more than the spoken word, and for the same reasons, should music be hurried.

For modern musicians, going back to the older instruments of the classical period constitutes first of all a process of un-learning, of abandoning a technique that is based on a high degree of tension. Even if a sense of frustration is experienced in the beginning (our tradition of a muscular approach is useless and damaging to the instrument and to the music), this first reaction is most often followed by a refreshing sense of freedom. Relaxation leads to elasticity; constant pressure is replaced by a multitude of differentiated impulses. And once these important principles have taken root in our way of interpreting the classical repertoire, it is certainly possible to achieve a workable compromise with modern instruments. In calligraphy the old quill pen is the ideal tool, but once we have mastered this art of beautiful writing and know how to differentiate the individual strokes, we will be able to produce artistic results even with a fountain pen.

> Jaap Schröder
> 'A performer's thoughts on
> Mozart's violin style'
> in *Perspectives on Mozart Performance*,
> ed. Larry Todd and
> Peter Williams, 1991

Mozart in literature

Mozart has been the subject of numerous works of literature, comic and tragic, from verse drama to prose narrative. The following extract is from 'Mozart and Salieri', one of the 'Little Tragedies' by the great Russian writer Alexander Pushkin.

Pushkin makes use of the idea, which originated with Mozart himself, that the composer was poisoned by his inferior rival, Antonio Salieri, in a fit of uncontrollable jealousy. Mozart is depicted as infuriatingly carefree and casual.

Scene 1
A room in Salieri's house

SALIERI

Justice, they say, does not exist on earth.
But justice won't be found in heaven either:
That's plain as any simple scale to me.
Born with a love of art, when as a child
I heard the lofty organ sound, I listened,
I listened and the sweet tears freely flowed.
Early in life I turned from vain
    amusements;
All studies that did not accord with music
I loathed, despised, rejected out of hand;
I gave myself to music. Hard as were
The earliest steps, and dull the earliest path,
I rose above reverses. Craftsmanship
I took to be a pedestal of art:
I made myself a craftsman, gave my fingers
Obedient, arid virtuosity. ...
I envy – I profoundly envy. Heaven!
O where is justice when the sacred gift,
Immortal genius, comes not in reward
For toil, devotion, prayer, self-sacrifice –
But shines instead inside a madcap's skull,
An idle hooligan's? O Mozart, Mozart!
                     (Enter Mozart.)

MOZART

You've seen me! – Damn! I have a joke for
    you –
I wanted to surprise you.

SALIERI

You here...

MOZART

Yes,
I came to show you something: on my way
I passed an inn, and there I heard a
    fiddle…
A funnier sound you never heard, Salieri –
A blind old tavern fiddler's 'Voi che sapete'!
Priceless! I couldn't help myself; I've
    brought him
To entertain you with his art. Come in!
        (Enter a blind old man with a violin.)
Something by Mozart, please.
        *(The old man plays an aria from 'Don
        Giovanni'. Mozart roars with laughter.)*

SALIERI

How can you laugh?

MOZART

How can you *not* laugh? Oh Salieri!

SALIERI

No:
I'm not amused when some appalling
    dauber
Tries his Raphael Madonna out on me,
I'm not amused when wretched
    mountebanks
Dishonour Dante with their parodies.
Be off, old man.

MOZART

Wait – drink my health with this.
        (Exit old man.)
You're out of sorts today, Salieri. Well,
I'll come another time.

SALIERI

What have you brought?

MOZART

Oh, nothing much. The other night
    insomnia
Plagued me again, some thoughts went
    through my head.
I wrote them down. I wanted your
    opinion…
You haven't time for me.

SALIERI

Oh Mozart! I –
No time for you? Sit down; I'm listening.

MOZART
                    (At the piano.)
Now,
Imagine…whom? – Myself, a little
    younger;
And I'm in love – not deeply, just a bit;
I'm with a pretty girl, or friend – say you,
I'm happy… Then: a vision of the grave,
Or sudden darkness, something of the kind.
Listen.
                            (Plays.)

SALIERI

You came to me with this, and stopped
To listen to a tavern scraper! Mozart,
You are unworthy of yourself.

MOZART

You like it?

SALIERI

What grace! What depth – what bold
    magnificence!
Mozart, you are a god: you do not know it,
But I know, I know.

MOZART

Nonsense! Well…who knows?
I'm starving though, in my divinity.

SALIERI

Let's dine together, come – the Golden
    Lion.

MOZART

Gladly. But first I'll have to tell my wife
I won't be home for supper.

Alexander Pushkin
Mozart and Salieri, 1830
Translated by Antony Wood, 1982

Theatre and cinema

In the 19th century Mozart had already become a subject for the stage. It was inevitable that in the 20th he would appear on the screen. However, the mixture of fact and fiction remains highly problematic.

In his play 'Amadeus' (first produced in London in 1979), Peter Shaffer like Pushkin explored the notion of the inexplicability, the 'undeserved' nature of genius. In both plays, Salieri nourishes a sense of injustice because the divine gift of music has been withheld from him and bestowed upon the carefree, worthless Mozart – 'beloved of God'. With that Shaffer combined the picture, put forward in Wolfgang Hildesheimer's biography of 1977, of Mozart's peculiar childlike psychology, and of Constanze's low character. The portrait was based to some extent on real documents, but it was distorted for theatrical effect, and one may regret that it has gained such wide currency – chiefly through Milos Forman's internationally successful film version (1984).

In Milos Forman's film version of Peter Shaffer's *Amadeus*, Mozart was played by Tom Hulce and Constanze by Elizabeth Berridge (left, their wedding), while F. Murray Abraham appeared as Salieri (top).

The operas, too, became the subject of films. The Swedish director Ingmar Bergman's 'Magic Flute' (1974), originally made for television, is a wonder-filled pantomime, part-comic and part-serious. Some scenes use the 18th-century theatre at Drottningholm near Stockholm, while others are entirely due to Bergman's visual imagination.

With his 'Don Giovanni' in 1979 Joseph Losey initiated a new wave of enormously popular film versions of operas, and Ruggiero Raimondi became a household name.

B elow: for the overture of *Don Giovanni,* Losey invented a fantastic sequence set in a Venetian glassworks, where Don Giovanni (Raimondi, wearing white in the centre) and the other characters stare into the furnace as into the flames of hell.

A bove: Pamina (Irma Urrila) and Tamino (Josef Kostlinger) undergo the trial by fire in Bergman's *Magic Flute.*

Year	Mozart	Literature and thought
1756	Born in Salzburg (27 January)	
1762	First travels (Munich, Vienna); first harpsichord compositions	J. J. Rousseau, *Emile* and *The Social Contract*
1763	To Paris	
1764	Arrives London (23 April)	
1765	Symphony no. 1. Leaves London (7 July); to Holland	Rousseau, *Confessions*
1768	*Bastien and Bastienne* (Vienna)	L. Sterne, *A Sentimental Journey*
1769	Departs for Italy (11 December)	
1770	Member of Accademia Filarmonica of Bologna First string quartet, K.80; *Mitridates* (Milan). In Rome, writes out Allegri's *Miserere* from memory	F. Hölderlin, W. Wordsworth, G. W. F. Hegel born
1771	*Ascanio in Alba* (Milan) Siegmund von Schrattenbach, Archbishop of Salzburg, dies	Sir W. Scott born
1772	Hieronymus Colloredo elected Archbishop of Salzburg Symphonies nos. 15–21; *Lucio Silla* (Milan)	S. T. Coleridge born
1773	Returns to Salzburg *Exsultate, jubilate*; String Quartets nos. 2–7 (Italy); String Quartets nos. 8–13 (Vienna); Piano Concerto no. 5; Symphonies nos. 25 and 28 (Salzburg)	O. Goldsmith, *She Stoops to Conquer*
1774	Symphony no. 29; Piano Sonatas nos. 1–5 (Salzburg)	J. W. von Goethe, *Werther*
1775	*La finta giardiniera* (Munich); Violin Concertos nos. 1–5 (Salzburg)	P. A. C. de Beaumarchais, *The Barber of Seville*; R. B. Sheridan, *The Rivals*
1776	*Serenata notturna*, K.239; *Haffner* Serenade, K.250 (Salzburg)	
1777	Piano Concerto no. 9 (Salzburg) Resigns his post as Kapellmeister and leaves Salzburg with his mother (23 Sept.); Munich, Augsburg, Mannheim	Sheridan, *The School for Scandal*
1778	Visits Kirchheim-Bolanden; falls in love with Aloysia Weber; arrives Paris (23 March) Concerto for Flute and Harp, K.299; Symphony no. 31, *Paris*; Piano Sonatas nos. 8 and 11 His mother dies in Paris (3 July)	Voltaire and Rousseau die
1781	*Idomeneo* (Munich); Serenade no. 10 Summoned to Vienna to join Colloredo; breaks with him. Lodges with Webers	J. C. F. von Schiller, *The Robbers*; E. Kant, *A Critique of Pure Reason*
1782	Adaptations of fugues by J. S. Bach; *The Abduction from the Seraglio* (Vienna); Symphony no. 35, *Haffner* (Vienna) Marries Constanze Weber (4 Aug.) First of the six 'Haydn' quartets, K.387	P. A. F. C. de Laclos, *Les Liaisons dangereuses*; F. Burney, *Cecilia*
1783	Mass in C minor, K.427; Symphony no. 36, *Linz* (Linz)	

Music	Visual arts	History
L. Mozart, *Violin Method*		Seven Years War begins
C. W. Gluck, *Orfeo and Euridice*; T. Arne, *Artaxerxes*	Petit Trianon, Versailles, begun	Accession of Catherine the Great in Russia
		Joseph II becomes Holy Roman Emperor
J. Haydn, Symphony no. 49, *La Passione*	Royal Academy of Arts, London, founded	
	Royal Crescent, Bath, completed	Napoleon and Wellington born J. Watt invents steam engine
L. van Beethoven born Gluck, *Paris and Helen*; A. Salieri, *Don Quixote*	F. Boucher and G. B. Tiepolo die T. Gainsborough, *The Blue Boy*; B. West, *Death of Wolfe*	Capt. Cook lands in Botany Bay
A. E. M. Grétry, *Zemire and Azor*		
Haydn, *Sun* Quartets, Symphony no. 45, *Farewell*		First partition of Poland
Haydn, *L'infedeltà delusa*		Boston Tea Party
Gluck, *Iphigenia in Aulis*		Accession of Louis XVI in France
	J. M. W. Turner and T. Girtin born	
E. T. A. Hoffmann born	J. Constable born	American Declaration of Independence
Gluck, *Armide*		
	G. B. Piranesi dies	France enters American War against Britain War between Austria and Prussia
N. Piccinni, *Iphigenia in Tauris*		
G. Paisiello, *The Barber of Seville*		
		End of American War of Independence

Year	Mozart	Literature and thought
1784	Piano Concertos nos. 14–18 Becomes a Freemason	Beaumarchais, *The Marriage of Figaro*
1785	Finishes the six quartets dedicated to Haydn. Piano concertos nos. 20 and 21; *Masonic Funeral Music*, K.477	Schiller, *Hymn to Joy*
1786	*The Impresario* (Schönbrunn); *The Marriage of Figaro* (Vienna)	
1787	To Prague Symphony no. 38, *Prague*; String Quintets K.515 and K.516 (Vienna); Serenade no. 13, *Eine kleine Nachtmusik* (Vienna); *Don Giovanni* (Prague) Leopold Mozart dies (28 May)	Schiller, *Don Carlos*; Goethe, *Iphigenia* Byron born
1788	Piano Concerto no. 26, *Coronation* (Vienna); Vienna premiere of *Don Giovanni*; Symphonies nos. 39–41	Kant, *A Critique of Practical Reason*
1789	Visits Prague, Dresden, Leipzig, Berlin Clarinet Quintet, K.581	C. Burney, *A General History of Music* completed
1790	*Così fan tutte* (Vienna)	Goethe, *Faust* (fragment)
1791	Piano Concerto no. 27 (Vienna); *La clemenza di Tito* (Prague); *The Magic Flute* (Vienna); Clarinet Concerto, K.622 (Vienna); *Requiem* Dies in Vienna (5 Dec.)	J. Boswell, *Life of Johnson*; D. A. F. de Sade, *Justine*

FURTHER READING

Documentary material

Emily Anderson, ed., *Letters of Mozart and his Family*, rev. 3rd edn, ed. S. Sadie and F. Smart, 1985
O. E. Deutsch, *Mozart, a Documentary Biography*, trans. E. Blom, P. Branscombe and J. Noble, 2nd edn, 1966
H. C. Robbins Landon, ed., *The Mozart Compendium*, 1991

General

Eric Blom, *Mozart*, 1955
Alfred Einstein, *Mozart: his Character, his Work*, trans. A. Mendel and N. Broder, 1946
Wolfgang Hildesheimer, *Mozart*, trans. M. Faber, 1983
H. C. Robbins Landon, *1791: Mozart's Last Year*, 1988
—— *Mozart, The Golden Years*, 1989
—— *Mozart and Vienna*, 1991
—— *Mozart and the Masons*, 1992

Early accounts

Lorenzo Da Ponte, *Memoirs*, 1828, trans. L. A. Sheppard, 1929
Edward Holmes, *The Life of Mozart including his Correspondence*, 1845

Michael Kelly, *Reminiscences*, 1826, new edn by Roger Fiske, 1975
Vincent and Mary Novello, *A Mozart Pilgrimage: being the Travel Diaries of Vincent and Mary Novello in the year 1829*, ed. N. Medici di Marignano and R. Hughes, 1955 and 1975

On opera

Peter Branscombe, *Die Zauberflöte*, 1991
E. J. Dent, *Mozart's Operas: a Critical Study*, 3rd edn, 1955
William Mann, *The Operas of Mozart*, 1977

Technical

Eva and Paul Badura-Skoda, *Interpreting Mozart on the Keyboard*, 1962
C. M. Girdlestone, *Mozart's Piano Concertos*, 1948
Charles Rosen, *The Classical Style*, 1971
L. Todd and P. Williams, eds., *Perspectives on Mozart Performance*, 1991

In other languages

Brigitte and Jean Massin, *Mozart*, 1958
Emmanuel Buenzod, *Mozart*, 1930
Mozart. Briefe und Aufzeichnungen. Gesamtausgabe, ed. W. A. Bauer and O. E. Deutsch, 1962
G. N. von Nissen, *Biographie W. A. Mozarts*, ed. Constanze (Mozart) Nissen, 1828, repr. 1964
Lotte Reiniger, *Mozart, die grossen Opern, mit Scherenschnitten*, 1987

Music	Visual arts	History
Salieri, *The Danaids*; Grétry, *Richard Coeur de Lion*		
S. Storace, *Gli sposi malcontenti*	Gainsborough, *The Morning Walk* J. L. David, *The Oath of the Horatii*	'Diamond Necklace' affair in France discredits Marie Antoinette
V. Martin y Soler, *Una cosa rara*; A. M. G. Sacchini, *Oedipus at Colonus*		Frederick the Great of Prussia dies; accession of Frederick William II
Salieri, *Tarare* M. L. Cherubini, *Demophon*		Joseph II abolishes capital punishment in Austria
Cherubini, *Iphigenia in Aulis*		Meeting of French Estates General *The Times* of London first appears
Paisiello, *Nina*	Brandenburg Gate, Berlin, begun	Storming of the Bastille; French declaration of human rights
		Joseph II dies; accession of Leopold II
Haydn, Symphony no. 94, *Surprise*		First French constitution

DISCOGRAPHY

Clarinet Concerto K.622
Antony Pay, Academy of Ancient Music, cond. Hogwood (Oiseau-Lyre). Karl Leister, Berlin Philharmonic Orchestra, cond. Karajan (EMI): the Berlin magic.

Clarinet Quintet K.581
Alan Hacker, Salomon Quartet (Amon Ra/Saydisc): a fine interpretation, on period instruments.

Così fan tutte
Schwarzkopf, Merriman, Otto, Simoneau, Panerai, Bruscantini, Philharmonia, cond. Karajan (EMI): captures the Italian verve of the opera and the charm of the young Schwarzkopf.

Don Giovanni
Schwarzkopf, Sutherland, Sciutti, Waechter, Taddei, Alva, Cappuccilli, Frick, Philharmonia, cond. Giulini (EMI): strikes the perfect balance between *dramma* and *giocoso*.

Flute Concerto K.313 and Concerto for Flute and Harp K.299
Jean-Pierre Rampal, Vienna Symphony Orchestra, cond. Guschlbauer (Erato), with Lily Laskine and Jean-François Paillard Ensemble for *Concerto for Flute and Harp* (Erato).

'Haffner' Serenade, K.250
Dresden Staatskapelle, cond. Harnoncourt (Teldec).

Horn Concertos
Dennis Brain, Philharmonia, cond. Karajan (EMI): a historic recording, still the most poetic.

Idomeneo
Hollweg, Schmidt, Palmer, Yakar, Equiluz, Zurich Opera House Mozart Orchestra, cond. Harnoncourt (Teldec): *opera seria* transfigured by lively, dramatic direction.

The Magic Flute
Dermota, Seefried, Kunz, Lipp, Loose, Weber, Vienna State Opera Chorus, Vienna Philharmonic Orchestra, cond. Karajan (EMI): a miracle of poetry. Salminen, Blochwitz, Hampson, Gruberova, Bonney, Scharinger, Zurich Opera Chorus and Orchestra, cond. Harnoncourt (Teldec).

The Marriage of Figaro
Della Casa, Gueden, Danco, Poell, Siepi, Dickie, Corena, Vienna Philharmonic Orchestra, cond. Kleiber (Decca): an inspired conductor and wonderful teamwork in the cast. Also worth considering are Karajan, with Schwarzkopf, and Muti (both EMI).

Mass in C Minor, K.427
Hendricks, Perry, Schreier, Luxon, Vienna Singverein, Berlin Philharmonic Orchestra, cond. Karajan (DG).

Piano Concertos

Complete: Daniel Barenboim, English Chamber Orchestra (EMI). Murray Perahia, English Chamber Orchestra (CBS). Two great artists at their peak.

Piano Sonatas
Complete: Daniel Barenboim (EMI). Individual sonatas: Maria João Pires, Mitsuko Uchida, Clara Haskil, Paul Badura-Skoda, Claudio Arrau, Alfred Brendel, Edwin Fischer.

Requiem
Mathis, Hamari, Ochman, Ridderbusch, Vienna State Opera Choir, Vienna Philharmonic Orchestra, cond. Böhm (DG).

The Seraglio
Rothenberger, Popp, Gedda, Unger, Frick, Vienna Philharmonic Orchestra, cond. Krips (EMI): humour and tenderness in the great Viennese tradition. Also the historic Beecham recordings (EMI).

Serenade for 13 Wind Instruments, K.361
Vienna Mozart Wind Ensemble, cond. Harnoncourt (Teldec): a vital new interpretation.

String Quartets
Complete: Amadeus Quartet (DG).
String Quintets K.174, 406, 515, 516, 593, 614
Complete: Budapest Quartet, Walter Trampler (CBS).
Symphonies
Complete: Academy of Ancient Music, cond. Schröder, Hogwood (Oiseau-Lyre), for those seeking performance on period instruments. Otherwise, perhaps here more than anywhere, selection is invidious. Classic recordings include those by Klemperer, Walter, Böhm, Jochum, Szell.
Violin Concertos K.207, 211, 216, 218, 219
Complete: Itzhak Perlman, Vienna Philharmonic Orchestra, cond. Levine (DG). Josef Suk, Prague Chamber Orchestra, cond. Hlavácek (Supraphon/Eurodisc).
Violin Sonatas nos. 20, 24 and 30, 25-8, 32 and 33
Itzhak Perlman, Daniel Barenboim (DG): perfect coexistence.

LIST OF ILLUSTRATIONS

The following abbreviations have been used: *a* above, *b* below, *c* centre, *l* left, *r* right; *Encyclopédie* = D. Diderot and J. d'Alembert, *Encyclopédie, ou Dictionnaire raisonné des sciences, des arts et des métiers*, Paris 1751–80; HMSW = Historisches Museum der Stadt Wien, Vienna; SM = Mozarteum, Salzburg

COVER

OPENING

CHAPTER 1

Painting, mid-19th c. Private coll.
128 J. M. Moreau, *Perfect Harmony.* Engraving, *c.* 1770. Bibliothèque des Arts Décoratifs, Paris

DOCUMENTS

INDEX

PHOTO CREDITS

All rights reserved 59, 60-1, 62-3, 68, 71*a*, 72-3*b*, 73*b*, 77*r*, 78, 84, 86-9, 97, 117*b*, 118*a*, 168, 172. Archiv für Kunst und Geschichte, Berlin 12, 13, 14-5*a*, 24, 26*a*, 27*a*, 32*a*, 36*a*, 37*al*, 37*ar*, 46*b*, 50, 51, 58, 66, 68-9*a*, 91*a*, 95, 96-7, 98, 100, 107, 108-9*b*, 110*b*, 112, 120-1, 122-3, 124-5, 152, 173. Artephot/Bibliothèque Nationale, Paris 94*b*. Artephot/Mandel, Paris 162. Artephot/Nimatallah, Paris 20-3. Artephot/O'Hana, Paris 53*a*, 53*b*. Artephot/Percheron 54-5. Harry R. Beard Coll., Theatre Museum, London 147. Bibliothèque Nationale, Paris 74*b*, 126-7*a*, 171. Bildarchiv der Österreichischen Nationalbibliothek, Vienna 101*b*, 138, 166. British Film Institute Stills, Posters and Designs, London 181*a*. Cahiers du Cinéma, Paris 178. Charmet, Paris 24-5. Dagli-Orti, Paris 18, 26*b*, 31, 36-7, 49, 67, 73*a*, 92-3, 102-3, 104-5, 116-7, 118*b*, 119*a*, 121*r*, 123*r*. Edimedia, Paris 72-3*a*. Enguerand, Paris 157. E. T. Archive, London 15, 48, 60, 61, 91*b*, 93. Explorer Archives, Paris 30*b*, 94*a*, 110*a*. Fayer, Vienna 174. Giraudon, Paris, 27*b*, 33, 100-1, 115*a*. Giraudon/Lauros, Paris 70. Greater London Photograph Library 143. Heliopolis Verlag, Tübingen 1-9, 116*l*, 117*ar*. Emily Lane 163. Magnum/Erich Lessing, Paris 14*l*, 16, 17, 38, 52, 68-9*b*, 80-1, 99, 106, 113, 114, 119*b*. Mozarteum, Salzburg 17, 19, 35, 133, 176. Municipal Museum, Salzburg front cover, 64, 105, 131. Musée Carnavalet, Paris 78-9. National Gallery, London 140. Réunion des Musées Nationaux, Paris 28-9, 39, 44-5, 63, 76, 77. Roger-Viollet, Paris 30*a*, 34, 40-1, 54*a*, 126-7*b*, 133, 136-7, 146, 155, 157. Royal College of Music, London 130. Scala, Florence 11, 32-3, 42, 43*b*, 56-7, 85, 90. Theatermuseum, Munich front cover, 154. Top/J. P. Charbonnier, Paris 158. Victoria and Albert Museum, London (photo Eileen Tweedy) 150.

TEXT CREDITS

Acknowledgment is gratefully made for use of material from Eva and Paul Badura-Skoda, *Interpreting Mozart on the Keyboard*, Barrie and Rockliff, London, 1962; Sir Thomas Beecham, *A Mingled Chime*, Hutchinson, London, 1944, reproduced with the permission of Shirley, Lady Beecham; Eric Blom's chapter on Mozart in Ralph Hill, *The Symphony*, Harmondsworth, 1949, reproduced by permission of Penguin Books Ltd; Alfred Einstein, *Mozart: his Character, his Work*, trans. Arthur Mendel and Nathan Broder, Cassell and Co., London, 1946; H. C. Robbins Landon, *1791: Mozart's Last Year*, Thames and Hudson, London, and Macmillan, New York, 1988; Alexander Pushkin, *Mozart and Salieri: The Little Tragedies*, trans. Antony Wood, 1982, 2nd revised edition, Angel Books, London and Dufour Editions, Chester Springs, Pa., 1987; Charles Rosen, *The Classical Style*, Copyright © 1971 by Charles Rosen, used by permission of Faber and Faber and of Viking Penguin, a division of Penguin Books USA Inc.; Artur Schnabel, *My Life and Music*, Longmans, Green and Co., London, 1961; Jaap Schröder's essay in Larry Todd and Peter Williams, eds, *Perspectives on Mozart Performance*, Cambridge University Press, 1991; Bernard Shaw, *Shaw's Music*, ed. Dan H. Lawrence, in *The Bodley Head Bernard Shaw*, The Bodley Head, London, 1981, by permission of the Society of Authors on behalf of the Bernard Shaw Estate.

Michel Parouty,
born in 1945, has an arts degree
and further qualifications in philosophy and
musicology from the universities of Poitiers and
Bordeaux. After spending some time as a teacher he
turned to journalism in 1979, joining the staff of
Opera International. He is now joint chief editor of
the French classical music magazine *Diapason*, and
has been a contributor to many international
publications including *L'Avant-Scène Opéra*,
L'Alphée, Monsalvat, Opera Canada, Scènes
magazines, Acte I Magazine, L'Evénement du jeudi
and the Swiss newspaper *La Tribune de Genève*. He
is co-author of a guide to symphonic music
published in 1986 and has just brought out
an edition of *La Traviata* in France.

© 1988 Gallimard
English translation © Thames and Hudson Ltd.,
London, and Harry N. Abrams, Inc., New York,
1993

Translated by Celia Skrine

Printed and bound in Italy by
Editoriale Libraria, Trieste